SUTTON POCKET HISTORIES

THE
EUROPEAN
UNION

MICHAEL MACLAY

SUTTON PUBLISHING

First published in the United Kingdom in 1998 by
Sutton Publishing Limited · Phoenix Mill
Thrupp · Stroud · Gloucestershire · GL5 2BU

British Library Cataloguing in Publication Data
A catalogue record for this book is available from the British
Library.

ISBN 0-7509-1952-3

Cover photograph by Andreas Rudolf (Tony Stone Images).

 ALAN SUTTON™ and SUTTON™ are the
trade marks of Sutton Publishing Limited

Typeset in 11/16 pt Baskerville.
Typesetting and origination by
Sutton Publishing Limited.
Printed in Great Britain by
The Guernsey Press Company Limited,
Guernsey, Channel Islands.

Contents

For Catriona and Christopher

Preface

In 1958, just as the European Community was being established, a letter arrived at its Brussels headquarters from an African businessman. 'We understand you are setting up a European common market,' the letter said. It went on 'We think this is a good idea. Could you please send us six copies of your catalogue. . . .'

Whatever agonizing and dissension there has been in the process of building up what has become the European Union, those on the outside have generally seemed to embrace its logic more willingly than those within. This has been as true of those far off, from the US to China, as of those closer in, the Central, Eastern and Southern Europeans who are nearly all jostling with one another to become members.

Yet the 'catalogue', the prospectus maybe, is not any more finished or definitive now than it was in the 1950s. Most of the countries of what is now the EU are embarking on their riskiest venture yet with the Single Currency and a successful outcome is by no means guaranteed. Still less do we know what deeper political integration might flow from a successful monetary union. But we can be clear by now that European Union is a dynamic process.

It is not, however, a predictable, linear process. What is often described on the continent as the 'construction of Europe', its policies as much as its institutions, has always embodied a tension between on the one hand what states thought they could do best by working together and pooling their resources and what on the other they felt, selfishly or sensibly, they must do themselves.

There has been a continuing dialogue, according to Jean Monnet's elegant formulation, between the collective and the individuals; in plainer speech, a continuing 'slugging match' involving both shared goals and national interests, in which each of the players without exception has exploited the shared goals when it suited to promote their own national advantage.

National motives have thus run in tandem with more collectivist notions of the common good at every turn of the wheel. In that way, the history of the EU is not dramatically different from other episodes of history, British or European. And we cannot tell how it will end. This means it has all the ingredients of a good story. Or of a good drama. If those of us in Britain understand the earlier acts a bit better, we might also be able to play our own role rather more effectively in future – whatever we may decide that role should be.

Acknowledgements

I am grateful to a number of politicians and officials, serving and retired, who have been generous with their time, insights and recollections. My thanks also to friends, family and colleagues who read through the draft, in particular to Richard Mayne, who was encouraging, kind and reproving in perfect measure.

List of Dates

1945   **13 May**. VE-Day (Victory in Europe)
       26 July. Clement Attlee's Labour government replaces
       Churchill's Tory administration
1946   **5 March**. Churchill's 'Iron Curtain' speech in Fulton,
       Missouri
       19 September. Churchill's Zürich speech
1947   **1 February**. De Gasperi Prime Minister in Italy
       17 March. Dunkirk Treaty between UK and France
       5 June. US Secretary of State Marshall's Harvard speech
       12–13 July. Paris agreement on Marshall economic
       recovery plan
1948   **22 January**. Bevin's 'Third Force' speech in House of
       Commons
       17 March. Brussels Treaty: UK, France and Benelux
       countries
       18 June. Berlin blockade
1949   **4 April**. North Atlantic Treaty signed
       5 May. Council of Europe set up in London
       8 August. First meeting of Council of Europe in
       Strasbourg
       15 September. Adenauer first Chancellor of German
       Federal Republic (FRG)
1950   **9 May**. Schuman Declaration

24 October. French Prime Minister René Pleven puts
forward plan to create an integrated European army

1951   **19 March**. European Coal and Steel Community (ECSC)
established in Paris, to include France, FRG, Italy,
Netherlands, Belgium and Luxembourg
18 April. Treaty of Paris signed

1952   **27 May**. Treaty for European Defence Community (EDC)
signed
10 August. ECSC High Authority starts work under
Presidency of Monnet

1953   **5 March**. Death of Stalin

1954   **30 August**. French assembly reject EDC
23 October. Establishment of Western European Union

1955   **1–2 June**. Messina meeting of Foreign Ministers of the Six
7 November. UK delegate Bretherton withdrawn from
Brussels talks

1957   **25 March**. Treaties of Rome establish EEC and EURATOM

1958   **29 May**. De Gaulle asked to form government in France

1960   **4 January**. European Free Trade Association (EFTA) set
up to include UK, Austria, Denmark, Norway, Portugal,
Sweden and Switzerland

1961   **10 August**. UK application to join EEC
17 August. Berlin Wall
10 November. Fouchet Committee proposals on political
union

1962   **17 April**. Negotiations on political union abandoned
30 July. Common Agricultural Policy operational
21 December. Nassau meeting between Macmillan and
Kennedy

1963 **14 January**. De Gaulle press conference rejecting UK membership of EEC

22 January. Elysée Treaty between France and FRG

29 January. End of UK membership negotiations

1965 **8 April**. Merger Treaty bringing together EEC, ECSC and EURATOM

2 July. De Gaulle boycott of EEC institutions

1966 **29 January**. Luxembourg compromise ends French 'empty chair' policy

10 March. De Gaulle takes France out of NATO

24 July. EEC agreement on CAP

1967 **10 May**. UK and Ireland renew membership application for EEC

27 November. Second de Gaulle veto

1968 **3 May**. Student revolt in Paris

30 June. De Gaulle election victory

1 July. Abolition of EEC customs duties; common external tariff

20 August. Soviets invade Czechoslovakia

1969 **28 April**. De Gaulle resigns

15 June. Pompidou becomes French President

21 October. Brandt FRG Chancellor

1–2 December. EEC Summit at The Hague

1970 **18 June**. Edward Heath replaces Wilson as UK Prime Minister

30 June. Start of EEC negotiations with UK, Denmark, Ireland and Norway

8 October. Werner Plan on economic and monetary union

27 October. Davignon Report on European political co-operation (EPC)

1972 **22 January**. Accession Treaties signed with UK, Denmark, Ireland and Norway

13 July. House of Commons approves UK accession

1973 **1 January**. EC formally enlarged to nine members. EC granted sole responsibility for common trade policy

1975 **5 June**. UK referendum votes to stay in EC

1977 **27 October**. Roy Jenkins, President of the Commission, launches EMU proposal in Florence

1981 **1 January**. Greece becomes tenth Member State

1983 **17–19 June**. European Council signs Solemn Declaration on European Union in Stuttgart

1984 **25–6 June**. Fontainebleau European Council reaches budget agreement to end dispute over UK contribution; sets up Dooge Committee

1985 **7 January**. Jacques Delors President of EC Commission

28–9 June. Milan European Council convenes Intergovernmental Conference (IGC) to amend Treaty of Rome

1986 **1 January**. Spain and Portugal join Community

17 and 28 February. Single European Act signed by governments of the twelve Member States

1987 **1 July**. Single European Act enters into force

1989 **26–7 June**. Madrid European Council agrees to convene IGC on economic and monetary union in line with 'Delors Plan'

1990 **1 July**. Stage One of economic and monetary union (EMU)

8 October. UK joins Exchange Rate Mechanism (ERM) of the EMS

22 November. Resignation of Mrs Thatcher; replaced by John Major

1991   **9–10 December**. European Council in Maastricht: heads of state or government agree draft Treaty on European Union

16 December. Europe Agreements signed by EC with Poland, Hungary and Czechoslovakia

1992   **7 February**. Maastricht Treaty on European Union signed

2 June. In a referendum 50.7 per cent of Danes vote against ratification of Maastricht Treaty

18 June. 67 per cent vote for Maastricht in referendum in Ireland

16 September. Pound sterling forced out of ERM on 'Black Wednesday'

20 September. 51.05 per cent of French vote in favour of Maastricht ratification

11–12 December. Edinburgh European Council agrees new arrangements for Denmark and endorses Delors 2 budget package

1993   **18 May**. 56.8 per cent of Danes vote in favour of Maastricht Treaty

2 August. French franc and ERM saved from speculative attacks by Bundesbank support and 'broad band' changes to ERM

1 November. Maastricht Treaty on European Union enters into force

1994   **1 January** Stage Two of EMU

1995   **1 January**. Austria, Finland and Sweden join EU

23 January. Jacques Santer succeeds Delors as Commission President

26–7 June. Cannes European Council mandates reflection group to prepare 1996 IGC on revision of Maastricht Treaty

15–16 December. Madrid European Council agrees on Euro as name for single European currency

1996 **29 March**. IGC on revision of Maastricht Treaty opened in Turin

13–14 December. European Council in Dublin agrees a stability and growth pact for the economic and monetary union

1998 **17 June**. Treaty of Amsterdam

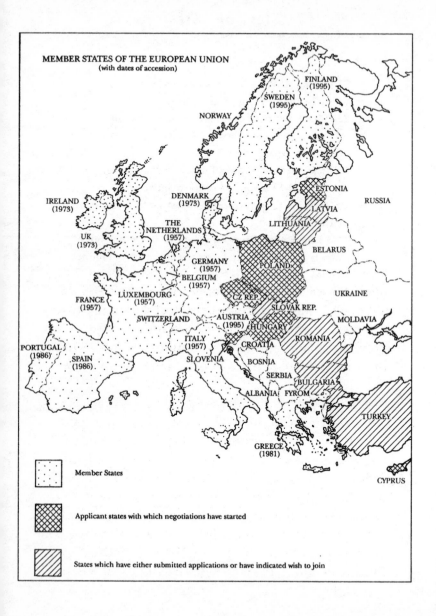

MEMBER STATES OF THE EUROPEAN UNION
(with dates of accession)

FINLAND (1995)
SWEDEN (1995)
NORWAY
ESTONIA
LATVIA
RUSSIA
DENMARK (1973)
LITHUANIA
IRELAND (1973)
THE NETHERLANDS (1957)
UK (1973)
BELARUS
GERMANY (1957)
POLAND
BELGIUM (1957)
CZ REP.
UKRAINE
FRANCE (1957)
LUXEMBOURG (1957)
SLOVAK REP.
SWITZERLAND
AUSTRIA (1995)
HUNGARY
MOLDAVIA
ITALY (1957)
CROATIA
ROMANIA
PORTUGAL (1986)
SPAIN (1986)
SLOVENIA
BOSNIA
SERBIA
BULGARIA
ALBANIA
FYROM
TURKEY
GREECE (1981)
CYPRUS

Member States

Applicant states with which negotiations have started

States which have either submitted applications or have indicated wish to join

ONE

Origins: Zürich to Strasbourg, 1945–9

The idea of European Union has been around in one form or another for longer than Christendom, although it was only from the sixteenth century that serious thought was given to portraying Europe as a political community or a community of law. What practical attempts there were to 'unify' Europe took the form of military expansionism, initially by dynasties such as the Bourbons or the Habsburgs and later by increasingly self-confident nation states starting with Napoleon's France. There were the beginnings of a sort of European *system* with the Concert of Europe in the early nineteenth century, but this did not survive long because it was too much associated with the conservative political programme of its main sponsor, Prince Metternich of Austria. The more idealistic schemes for European unity, from the poetic flights of Victor

1

Hugo to the grand plans of Tsar Alexander III of Russia, either stayed in the world of ideas or were ground down into specific and occasionally constructive innovations like the International Court in The Hague in 1903.

During the course of the First World War, German strategists sketched out plans for the sort of Europe that they thought would be able to hold its own economically against the superpowers they already saw taking shape in America and Russia. And in the interwar period there was co-operation across borders between French, German and other European steel producers, which foreshadowed the sort of economic pooling of resources that would take place in the 1950s. But the greater legacy of the awfulness of war was a tradition of idealism whose finest if most flawed product was the League of Nations. One of the most high-flown speeches heard in the grandiose headquarters of the League in Geneva was the proposal in 1929, by the French statesman Aristide Briand, for 'a system of European Federal Union', a proposal as vivid and visionary as it was hopelessly mistimed, just ahead of the world financial crash and the rise of the Nazis in Germany.

Yet, in the course of the Second World War, the concepts of federalism that had been pioneered by colourful individuals like the Marquess of Lothian and Count Richard Coudenhove-Kalergi attracted a broader following. For refugees from defeated nations, such as Paul-Henri Spaak of the Netherlands or Alcide De Gasperi from Italy, the postwar period would have to be about something other than reconstructing failed nation states and national economies, if the finest European values were to be upheld. One of the dominant figures of the era, Jean Monnet, came to this conclusion by a very practical route. Monnet had been Assistant Secretary-General of the League of Nations. He knew at first hand the inadequacy of good intentions and goodwill. But as a cognac salesman and banker by background, who played a key role in both world wars in organizing Anglo-French supply programmes, he had a very concrete rationale for believing in thorough-going co-operation across borders. It had been the key to survival in wartime. He believed that integration between nations and peoples would be equally indispensable to consolidate the security and prosperity of Europe in peacetime.

However, the devastated landscape of Europe in 1945 did not lend itself to generous international visions. In the struggle for economic survival and political coherence, the continental Western European countries dragging themselves back from defeat were not in any position to lead. With Soviet

Russia sitting alarmingly on the Eastern part of the continent and Western Europe dominated by American GIs and emergency assistance programmes, such moral leadership as there was within Europe came – even following Winston Churchill's replacement by Attlee's Labour government – from Britain.

As the brief euphoria at war's end was replaced by forebodings about Soviet intentions, it was Churchill himself who in September 1946, in Zürich, gave most eloquent expression to Europe's plight: 'Over wide areas a vast quivering mass of tormented, hungry, care-worn and bewildered human-beings gape at the ruins of their cities and homes, and scan the dark horizons for the approach of some new peril, tyranny or terror.' Churchill's answer was 'to re-create the European family, or as much of it as we can, and provide it with a structure under which it can dwell in peace, in safety and in freedom. We must build a kind of United States of Europe.'

Churchill's Zürich speech set him up as something of a patron saint for those who over the next two generations dedicated themselves to building up new institutions for a new Europe. Yet Churchill spoke as an opposition politician, out of office – as a revered statesman, and a man of bold literary and journalistic imagination, but not as a man who

would have to make a reality of his own brave words.
Even if he had been in power, Churchill would not
have put Britain at the head of the enterprise. He
certainly had no illusions about the implications of
his vision for national sovereignty: he went on to say
in his speech that the structure of the United States
of Europe, 'if well and truly built, will be such as to
make the material strength of a single state less
important'. But as he had said on another occasion,
though he carefully did not say in Zürich: 'We have
our own dream and our own task, we are *with*
Europe but not *of* it. We are linked but not
compromised.'

This is not to say he thought that Britain's task
excluded Europe. Churchill saw Britain's international role as lying at the intersection of three
circles: Empire, the Special Relationship with the
United States, and Europe. Ernest Bevin, who was
responsible for Britain's foreign policy under Attlee,
saw things in similar terms, even if his rhetoric was
different. When he assumed office, he spoke of the
need for a 'Third Force', a Western union which
would bring together Europe's states in an
economic, commercial and military alliance under
British leadership. This should be compatible with a
close alliance with the United States and with a
British Empire evolving under socialist leadership

into a Commonwealth of equals. Bevin returned to the theme in subsequent years, notably in January 1948 when he set out in the House of Commons an ambitious vision of his Third World Force as being the best protection for Europe against the Soviet threat. Having discussed this with the French government, Bevin believed that the British and French colonies, especially in Africa, could buttress rather than conflict with this European blueprint.

The problem with all of these plans was 'events', as Macmillan would ruefully observe later on. From the moment of Churchill's 'Iron Curtain' speech at Fulton, Missouri, in March 1946, the priority for Western diplomacy was how to respond to Stalin. The real punctuation points in the immediate postwar period were the failure to agree peace arrangements with the Soviets for Germany; the gradual absorption of Central and Eastern Europe, notably Hungary and Czechoslovakia, into the Soviet bloc; then the Berlin blockade and Britain's inability to resist communist advances in Greece. At the same time, Attlee's Cabinet was trying to manage the decolonization of India and becoming bogged down in events in Palestine. Taken together with a declining economic situation, punctuated by successive sterling crises – and even aggravated by bursts of the most calamitous winter weather in generations – Britain was not in a position to drive events in Europe.

This did not prevent the consolidation of friendship with France in the Dunkirk Treaty early in 1947. Following Bevin's powerful appeal for the Third Force, this was extended to Belgium, Luxembourg and the Netherlands in the Brussels Treaty of March 1948. But when US Secretary of State General George Marshall announced in June that year a huge programme of American assistance to help rebuild Europe's shattered economies, Britain had to choose whether it wanted the aid to be administered country by country or on the basis of a more integrated approach to the problems which the states of Europe faced.

The US favoured the establishment of a strong central organization to judge priorities, administering what became the European Recovery Programme on the basis of very close co-ordination between the recipients of aid. The British government, on the other hand, were determined that the direction from the centre should be weak. They vetoed the appointment of Paul-Henri Spaak, the outstanding candidate for Secretary-General of the new Organization for European Economic Cooperation (OEEC), on the grounds that he was too committed to a federal Europe. For as the implications of

Bevin's more exuberantly European ideas were thought through within the British policy machine, they ran into opposition. For instance, Bevin regularly raised the idea of a European customs union, dismantling trade barriers between states to boost commerce between them. This was opposed by the Colonial Office, which saw negative implications for trade with the colonies. It was also unpopular with other home departments: Duff Cooper, British Ambassador in Paris, memorably noted that 'the mere words "customs union" produce a shudder in the Treasury and nausea in the Board of Trade'.

As would be the case for succeeding generations in Britain, the idea of surrendering control of essential economic levers had powerful opponents. To be fair, it would have been difficult to foresee either the economic potential of Britain's European neighbours, still not far off subsistence at the time, or the fact that Britain's colonial possessions would ultimately be floated off into other economic spheres than the system of Imperial Preference in which they had for many years played a critical part.

At the same time, this period saw considerable political success in the way Britain managed the all-important commitment of the US to European defence. One of Bevin's personal, though probably erroneous, beliefs was that if Europe seemed too self-sufficient, this would encourage the strong isolationist tendencies in the US Administration and Congress to disengage the US from Europe. By committing Britain to European defence in the Brussels Treaty, he skilfully prepared a template which was filled out with the North Atlantic Treaty a year later, engaging the US and Canada in a way that would stand the test of time.

But by this point, the thrust of British policy in Europe was clear. A series of meetings between Jean Monnet and Sir Edwin Plowden, a key official in the management of the British economy, revealed the difference of approach. Monnet was at the time in charge of the Commissariat du Plan, the planning commission driving French economic recovery, and he wanted to explore with the British how they could work more closely together. He was particularly concerned about the rehabilitation of Germany into the wider European economy. Monnet had high expectations of the British government, hoping they would help form a nucleus around which a European community might be founded – and was deeply disappointed to observe that in reflecting the political will of the government, his interlocutors could not even begin to rise to his remarks.

A clear public symbol of Britain's commitment to co-operation between governments, rather than integration, came with the establishment of the Council of Europe. This was the organization which grew out of Churchill's campaign for European unity dating from his Zürich speech. Attlee's government had no enthusiasm for the idea. Bevin said in one of the great mixed metaphors of history: 'I don't like it. I don't like it. When you open that Pandora's Box you'll find it full of Trojan horses.' But seeing the importance it was assuming on the continent, the British government played along, encouraging a grand assembly of parliamentarians in The Hague in 1948, but ensuring that matters of substance were either addressed elsewhere, like defence which was discussed at NATO, or not at all, like economics which was excluded specifically from the Council's remit. In the event, the Council of Europe was established in Strasbourg in August 1949 under the chairmanship of Paul-Henri Spaak, and after a colourful start it evolved into a modest and civilized forum of discussion between governments and parliamentarians, doing useful work across a number of fields including culture, education and human rights. But this fell far short of the hopes invested in it by many people, especially in France and the Benelux countries.

Monnet was appalled. For the idealism and ambition not only of Churchill but of Spaak or de Gasperi to be channelled into what he saw as a talking-shop was for him a disgrace. He observed later: ' . . . it was nothing . . . it was a meeting of men of goodwill but with no power, no authority. It was a gathering of people, expressing general views and going home. But that is not *acting*, not taking decisions. . . . What we are trying to do is to create between the nations of Europe a *common interest*.'

Monnet had sterner ideas about how to move things forward. If Britain could not yet be part of it, he felt, so be it. Consolidating a common interest was going to require other partners.

TWO

Forging Integration: Paris to Rome, 1949–57

Jean Monnet was the opposite of the colourless cosmopolitan bureaucrat. He was firmly rooted in the gentle landscape of Cognac and his professional training was in the family wine and spirits business. But his father sent him to live with a wine merchant in London when he was sixteen. There he soaked up the confidence and dignity of Edwardian Britain. The admiration he felt for the way the British ran their society and institutions had an enduring effect on him. But Monnet also spent time doing business in North America, Germany and the Low Countries, as well as working in London to help the supply lines of the Franco-British war effort in the First World War. After his time at the League of Nations he helped the Chinese to reorganize their railways. He worked as a British civil servant in Washington during the Second World War and was more responsible than anyone else for the last-ditch proposal made by Churchill, as France fell to the Germans, for a Franco-British Union to prevent all of France's assets falling into German hands.

This was a man who understood the varieties of nations and nationhood. But all of his experience pointed him to the belief that nations would do their people most proud when they found ways of pooling their strengths. It was thus as an 'operator', someone who knew his way around governments and international organizations and who knew how to get at the levers of power, that he approached the French Prime Minister, Georges Bidault, and then the Foreign Minister, Schuman, with a proposal to integrate the coal and steel industries of Western Europe. The 40 per cent of Europe's iron and steel resources situated in the Ruhr were at the time under international administration. His proposal was that they, as well as the remaining coal and steel industries around Europe, should be brought together under a new European Coal and Steel Community run by a High Authority in Luxembourg. It was surely unthinkable that France and Germany would go to war again if their most basic industrial capacities were shared. By showing the merits of close co-operation in this fundamental sector, he hoped to set a precedent for integration in other areas of industry.

When Bidault failed to spark, it was Schuman who accepted the diagnosis of France's chief planner and announced the proposal as his own on 9 May 1950. The Germans had already been consulted and saw it as a fast track to their acceptance as an industrial partner to their erstwhile military foes. Chancellor Konrad Adenauer sent his discreet but enthusiastic encouragement. Similarly, the US Secretary of State, Dean Acheson, passing through Paris at the time, was let in on the secret and was duly impressed. However, Monnet wanted the British to be faced with the hard choice of accepting the basic principles of the plan, so that they could not derail the idea before it gathered speed. He still hoped he might get them on board, but the supranational elements in the proposal were very clear. British opposition was in the first instance inevitable.

Monnet envisaged a system under which tariffs and quotas between the Member States would be dismantled and common policies on prices, imports and subsidies introduced over time. Unfair competition would be illegal. Each Member State would have the advantage of direct access to the other's markets. In the event that there were crises in the coal or steel industries, they would consult together on the best ways of reducing production. Given the key importance of these industries, there would need to be in addition to the High Authority a Special Council of Ministers from the Member States, a Common Assembly of nominated Members of Parliament and an impartial Court of Justice for the settlement of disputes. It is uncanny in retrospect that Monnet's sketch for this first attempt at integration should have provided such a robust model for the subsequent development of the European Community.

But the blueprint was too ambitious in the first instance even for the Dutch, usually among the first enthusiasts for integration. They said they accepted the draft proposal as a basis for negotiation, but they reserved their right to retract if they were not satisfied with the execution of the principles. This was a cautious and pragmatic stance – in contrast to that of the British whose immediate response was simply to reject the proposal as too far-reaching. Bevin was furious with Acheson and with the French for keeping him in the dark. But his political view was clear: 'The Durham miners won't wear it', he remarked. The British government nevertheless offered to join discussions 'in a constructive spirit' in the hope that there would emerge another scheme which they could join.

Some serious attempts were made by the French to find a formulation which the British could accept as a way into the talks. But British ministers still refused to endorse what might be taken as prior commitment to the acceptance of supranational institutions. When the French government imposed a deadline for the British response, this further ruffled feathers both in London and at the embassy in Paris. There has been much discussion of whether if all the main ministers had been available at the time – which they were not – or if British officials had not been over-fastidious in their advice about prior commitments – as they probably were – the break could have been avoided. Churchill and the Conservative Opposition in the House of Commons were cutting in their criticism that the government should at least have exhausted discussion before deciding the gap was too wide. But it is difficult in retrospect to imagine the British swallowing their misgivings at this stage. Britain's own coal and steel industries were far greater than those of other European countries and the idea of giving power over British industries to an international body must have seemed novel and dangerous. When, on 3 June 1950, a joint communiqué was issued by the governments of France, Germany, Italy and the Benelux countries – the 'Six' – a pattern was set which would last for a generation.

The ECSC was quickly a success, following signa-ture of the Treaty of Paris in April 1951. Monnet became the first President of its High Authority. It enabled German production of coal and steel in particular to be increased dramatically but not in a way that was perceived as threatening by its neighbours. The Head of the British delegation to the ECSC in Luxembourg, Sir Cecil Weir, was quick to recognize its value, urging on London a more forthcoming attitude. Yet looking back some years later, Monnet told his assistant Richard Mayne that he thought he himself had made mistakes in thinking of ECSC as a power above nations, continually stressing the supranational element: 'What eventually emerged . . . was a dialogue between the independent body, which was the High Authority, and the Ministers representing the Nation States.' This dialogue became in his view the real motor of integration in Europe.

The next phase in Monnet's campaign to promote what was then his model of European union demonstrated that it simply would not occur if national politics were played wrong. The start of the Korean War in 1950 had revived US pressure on the Europeans to get their act together on defence. In particular they needed to find a way of enabling the Germans to rearm without terrifying their neighbours – shades of ECSC, and something the Dunkirk and Brussels treaties had not provided for.

Monnet was at the time flushed with success from progress on the Schuman plan, though the treaty had not yet been signed. He used basically the same team and the same way of doing things to provide the French Defence Minister, René Pleven, with a similar plan for a European Defence Community (EDC) that would enable German troops to be re-armed but under a European banner. It helped that Pleven had been one of Monnet's team during the war.

After Pleven announced his Plan in the French National Assembly on 23 October 1950, he ran into predictable rejection from the Russians – and from the British. But this story was going to be much more complicated than that of ECSC.

The US administration was initially unenthusiastic, preferring the direct recruitment into NATO of a German contingent – which the French did not like. It took a year to persuade the Americans of the merits of the EDC. But, as if in a game of Chinese whispers leading from Monnet to Eisenhower, Eisenhower to Acheson and from Acheson to the President, Harry Truman, the Americans were brought round. The Dutch, as with ECSC, needed to be convinced. But by dint of discussion and persuasion, they were. By May 1952 the same Six countries had signed up for a similar structure to

ECSC: an Executive Commissariat, a Council of Ministers, an Assembly and a Court. Seeing the huge implications of the scheme, the ECSC Council of Ministers asked for work to be done to create a European Political Community (EPC), which would hoist an umbrella of legitimacy over all of the integration efforts in progress. The draft treaty was amended accordingly. Maybe Churchill's United States of Europe would arrive sooner than he had anticipated.

But it was not to be. The treaty was ratified after long and earnest debate in the parliaments of the FRG and the Benelux countries. The Italians hesitated, still rather hoping that the British might negotiate their way back into the process. But it was in France that the treaty was to fail. There were strong opponents in the French National Assembly of the idea of German rearmament in any form, notably among the Gaullists and the Communists. There was further opposition to the huge leap into political union that was being anticipated. The helter-skelter succession of governments in the final days of the Fourth Republic also brought in defence ministers and prime ministers who were not so enamoured of the treaty as it had developed. It was Pierre Mendès-France, heading a coalition of Radicals and Gaullists, who made the final effort to negotiate the plan back into a shape he thought would be acceptable – essentially dropping the proposals for political union – and having failed, submitted the full treaty, including EDC and EPC, to the National Assembly. After making a lukewarm speech and abstaining himself, he was not surprised to see it go down, on 30 August 1954, by fifty-odd votes.

This provided the British with a welcome chance to play the 'good Europeans'. They shared US concern that the Germans should be brought back into play on military questions, and they very much wanted to control the European defence agenda – a consistent priority in Britain's European role. Anthony Eden, the Foreign Secretary, embarked on one of the first-ever episodes of shuttle diplomacy, between Paris, Bonn, Rome and Brussels. In the course of a few weeks he managed to sell to the Six and to the Americans his proposal for a Western European Union (WEU) that would extend the provisions of the Brussels Treaty to the FRG and Italy. The agreement was signed on 23 October 1954 in Paris and it brought an end to the occupation regime in Germany, as well as German renunciation of atomic, biological or chemical weapons, and a limit of twelve divisions on her land forces – welcome reassurance to the mistrustful French parliamentarians who had killed EDC. There was hardly a hint of supranational authority in the text of the treaty, though British commitment to the defence of continental Europe was firmed up.

Monnet's disappointed response was to announce that he would not seek re-election as President of the ECSC High Authority the following year. He set about a campaign of what we would now call intensive 'networking', and one of the fruits of this was to be his Action Committee for the United States of Europe (ACUSE), which was launched in October 1955. This was a high-profile pressure group for European integration, drawing on all the political parties and trade unions in the Six countries, except for the Communists, the Gaullists and the Italian neo-fascists. It also kept up with blue-chip contacts in and out of government on the other side of the Atlantic and provided a steady drumbeat of support and enthusiasm for a succession of European initiatives. Monnet himself, once described by a British diplomat as 'a mixture of gangster and conspirator', increasingly played a behind-the-scenes role as the politicians took the lead in what became the first 'relaunch' of Europe.

It was the Dutch Foreign Minister, Johan Willem Beyen, who formally moved things forward, speaking up for a customs union as the first step in creating an economic union. The idea was picked up by Luxembourg's Foreign Minister, Joseph Bech, and pulled together with further proposals from his Belgian and Dutch colleagues in a joint Benelux memorandum. This made a full-throated appeal for further integration in the fields of transport, energy and atomic power, as well as suggesting for the first time a 'European Economic Community'. The idea then gathered steam through some complicated horse-trading, with the French interested in collaboration on atomic power, the Germans keen on any wider scheme that would bring them into the mainstream, and Monnet himself pressing for the application of ECSC-type structures to further sectors of industry. Something from everyone was put in the pot. It was an early example of the Six agreeing on the 'highest common multiple' of ambitions, rather than seeking the 'lowest common denominator' of agreement which would have been the more logical, British way of proceeding. Whatever the complex parentage of the Benelux memorandum, it was Monnet who received a copy from the Belgian Foreign Minister, Paul-Henri Spaak, with a covering note saying 'Voici votre bébé', 'Here is your baby.'

Three weeks later, on 1 June 1955, representatives of the Six, mostly Foreign Ministers, met in Messina to thrash out a resolution which would take in the Benelux proposals and explore ways of putting them into effect. They finished over supper in the nearby monastery of San Domenico in Taormina, which gazes out on the Mediterranean from an idyllic hillside town of Greek, Roman and Norman ruins: historic in every sense. The French government had informally suggested that the British might wish to be represented. 'A devilish awkward place to expect a minister to get to', had been the equally informal response.

But the British government did send a representative to the meetings that now took place at a rustic country house outside Brussels under the forceful chairmanship of Paul-Henri Spaak. Russell Bretherton, an Under-Secretary from the Department of Trade, spent an uneasy few months attending detailed daily discussion of proposals of which his government had already said they disapproved. Alternating by all accounts between projecting a tone of sceptical enquiry and withdrawing behind his pipe, he was in an impossible position. The British government made clear its unhappiness at the course of events in September 1955 and, when the moment came for political decision, Bretherton withdrew, according to one distinguished French official, making a statement which encapsulates what must have been the uneasy mix of Britain's wishful thinking and awkward forebodings at the time:

> I have followed your work with interest, and sympathetically. I have to tell you that the future Treaty which you are discussing
> a) has no chance of being agreed
> b) if it were agreed, it would have no chance of being ratified
> c) if it were ratified, it would have no chance of being applied.
> And please note that if it were applied, it would be totally unacceptable to Britain. You speak of agriculture, which we don't like, of power over customs, which we take exception to, and of institutions, which horrifies us.
> Monsieur le président, messieurs, au revoir et bonne chance.

It has to be said that today a statement of such resonance seems almost too convincing to be true, at least as retailed in Jean François Deniau's powerful and poetic plea for European unity, 'Forbidden Europe'. There has never been another source for the story and Bretherton is almost certainly being done a historical injustice. But even if the statement was not quite delivered in this form, it undoubtedly contains the deeper truth of British policy at the time.

Without Bretherton, who certainly ceased to attend at Val Duchesse, the delegates now immersed themselves in the detail of what became an ever more ambitious scheme. The Spaak Report made recommendations for a common market, an integrated approach to priority sectors in Europe's economy and a new agency to deal with atomic energy. The institutional structure was based on that of ECSC.

Meanwhile, the British counter-attacked at the OEEC with their own initiative, the so-called Plan G, which aimed to create a wider free trade area without the supranational features. This at least had the merit of forcing the British to think about how a tariff-free Europe would work. But without the common discipline of a common external tariff, the idea was eventually dismissed, especially by the French, as a threat to dissolve the evolving European community 'like a lump of sugar in a British cup of tea'. Despite determined lobbying of the French, the Dutch and the Americans, the British government made no headway, whether by seduction or by sabotage, in undermining the will of the Six to go ahead. And they had to look on as observers as the Spaak Report was turned into legal language in time for an elaborate ceremony in the Capitol in Rome, on 25 March 1957, when the Treaties of Rome, establishing the European Economic Community (EEC) and the European Atomic Energy Community (EURATOM) were signed.

Looking back years later, Russell Bretherton was in no doubt that his neither-here-nor-there presence in Brussels, in line with his instructions, had been a mistake: 'If we had taken a firm line, that we wanted to come in and be a part of this, we could have made that body more or less into whatever we liked.' Spaak himself had indicated on many occasions that Britain possessed a moral quality which would have given it the leadership of any such initiative if it had only had the conviction. But whether this was still the case in the late 1950s, as the Six worked their own way through the possibilities, must remain open to doubt. More to the point was the view expressed on ECSC much earlier in the decade by Sir Cecil Weir: 'Sooner or later we will be presented with a choice between association by treaty or membership or shutting up shop here in Luxembourg as a major delegation exercising an effective and useful role . . . the longer we postpone such a decision, the more difficult it will be to secure entry on satisfactory terms.' This prescient observation was to be the underlying story of Britain's relationship with the European Communities as they took shape over the vital years that followed.

THREE

At Sixes and Sevens: Stockholm to The Hague, 1958–69

The Treaty of Rome came into force on 1 January 1958 and the first European Commission under Walter Hallstein of Germany took the lead in seeking to apply its provisions. The broad direction was indicated in the Treaty's preamble: 'to lay the foundations of an ever closer union among the peoples of Europe.' But for all the detailed aspirations contained in its 200 or so Articles, most of the policies to make it reality were only to be worked out over time.

One principle which Monnet had successfully entrenched and which had been spelt out in the Spaak report was that a real Community could only be created on the basis of 'common rules, joint action and finally an institutional system to watch over it'. In his memoirs Monnet stressed this cardinal belief: 'Nothing is possible without men; nothing is lasting without institutions.' It was the latter proposition that the British still found so intimidating.

The British Prime Minister at the time was Harold Macmillan. He saw himself as a European by conviction and still hoped that the Six could be brought around to accepting the looser free trade area being canvassed within the OEEC under his government's Plan G. His Paymaster-General, Reginald Maudling, conducted an energetic negotiation to this end in a committee formed with other national delegates. The prospects did not seem altogether bad when General Charles de Gaulle was invited to form a new French administration at the end of May 1958: de Gaulle made clear very quickly that he was a believer in the 'Europe des Etats', a Europe of sovereign states which was very different either from Monnet's federalist vision or from the views of the squabbling politicians who had led the crumbling Fourth Republic. The British also received signs from the Federal German Economics Minister, Ludwig Erhard, that some sections of German business opinion were sympathetic to their ideas on a free trade area.

However, in an early foreshadowing of the way the Franco-German alliance would drive Europe's agenda, de Gaulle and the Federal Chancellor, Konrad Adenauer, held their first meeting in Colombey-les-Deux-Eglises. They agreed that their priority was the solidarity of the existing Community of Six, whatever their goodwill towards other European countries. De Gaulle's lack of federalist inclinations did not mean he was a believer in free trade. At the increasingly tense meetings of Maudling's committee it became clear that the Germans would now back de Gaulle's defence of what he saw as their shared interests. Negotiations on Plan G were broken off in December 1958.

The British government now began discussions with six of the remaining members of the OEEC – Sweden, Norway and Denmark, Austria, Switzerland and Portugal – to set up a separate free trade organization. At the Stockholm Convention of 4 January 1960, representatives of the Seven signed the European Free Trade Area (EFTA) into existence. The idea was that this modest experiment in tariff cutting and loose government-to-government co-operation should act as a magnet for the countries of the Six, as they found the bureaucracy and regulation of the EEC burdensome, and conflicts between them became unavoidable.

Things turned out rather differently. It soon became clear that Britain had less to gain than its new partners from the small, relatively open markets of the Seven. The British economy was also weaker than was generally appreciated and soon lagged behind the economies of the Six, which were experiencing a powerful economic boom which lasted until the end of the 1960s. As the first EEC tariff cuts took effect in 1959, the British began to feel excluded from the markets that looked most promising for them, while their links with the Commonwealth began to throw up more problems than opportunities. Former colonial countries wanted increasingly to plot their own industrial strategies, while their desire to maintain their agricultural exports to Britain placed constraints on British domestic production.

Quite briskly, Macmillan commissioned a re-examination in Whitehall of the pros and cons of EEC membership. This was led by Sir Frank Lee, one of the towering public servants of the period who had just taken over the Treasury. By sheer force of intellect and energy, he persuaded long standing opponents of integration across government ministries that the balance of advantage now favoured British participation if the terms were right. For his part, Macmillan was within months of his dramatic 'Winds of Change' speech in Africa, preparing the political ground for a change of policy in Europe. In the summer of 1960 he reshuffled his Cabinet to put ministers he saw as pro-European, such as Lord Home, Edward Heath and Duncan Sandys, in the key positions. Rab Butler, the most important figure in the Conservative Party after Macmillan himself, was given a co-ordinating role in the course of which he convinced himself rather felicitously that the time had come to seek membership of what was now known in Britain as 'the Common Market'. In August 1961 an application to join was formally launched, with Edward Heath, the most convinced pro-European in the government, as chief negotiator.

The EEC was itself at a sensitive stage of evolution. While de Gaulle had initially left it to the Commission to work through the first stages of the commercial, industrial and agricultural reforms necessary, he increasingly wanted to shape the institutions according to his own vision. Following a dramatic press conference in September 1960 in which he stressed the ultimate authority of the Member States, he secured the appointment of an intergovernmental committee in early 1961 to examine ways to establish new forms of political co-operation – not integration – within the EEC. This had the paradoxical effect of frightening the other Five into enthusiasm for the idea of British membership, to counterbalance the power of the General, even though British views were closer to those of de Gaulle than to their own, more federalist preferences.

But de Gaulle's priority was to drive the EEC in a direction that would favour the interests of France. One of his ambassadors, Christian Fouchet, was put in charge of the intergovernmental committee, which presented a set of proposals envisaging a 'Union of States' to function alongside the existing Community, with responsibility for key areas like foreign policy, defence and culture. One important element in de Gaulle's thinking was to establish an international presence that would be independent of US influence, which he already saw as over dominant within the Alliance.

With the Germans and the Italians unhappy and the Benelux countries not wanting to see progress on these important questions until Britain was inside the Community, the Fouchet Committee was told to produce a second report. When this arrived in February 1962, it was seen as even worse than the first report. At the same time, the French brought the long-running negotiations over agricultural prices to a head, making clear that if they did not get agreement there would be a crisis of confidence in the Community. The upshot was that the agricultural deal was done, setting the pointers for agricultural price support for a generation, while the Fouchet Plan was to die a slow death, following adjournment of the committee's work in April. The Community had lost something of its innocence. The new balance of commitments and obligations was going to make British entry more difficult than the British themselves realized.

Following a long summer of detailed negotiations on industrial tariffs, agricultural prices and arrangements for the Commonwealth countries, the tide of opinion within Britain, which had been mildly positive, turned around. At the Labour Party Conference in October, the Opposition leader Hugh Gaitskell said a decision to join the Community would mark 'the end of a thousand years of history'. The popular press began to play up the difficulties for loyal Commonwealth countries if they were deserted by Britain. Although this did not undermine the government's strength of purpose in the negotiations, it did mean that Heath and his team had to err on the side of showing they were putting up a tough fight for British and Commonwealth interests. And this, in a further portent of things to come, had the effect of souring the atmosphere with their proposed Community partners.

Nevertheless, there was enough real progress on substantive questions that all of the Six apart from the French anticipated a successful outcome. The final hitch came from an unanticipated direction. For all his European credentials, Macmillan saw himself as a particular friend of the US, a wise and avuncular adviser to the young President, John F. Kennedy. His description of the British role as playing Greece to America's Rome was at best patronizing, and at worst irritated the Americans while infuriating the French. When Macmillan went to Nassau in the Bahamas in December 1962 to discuss the future of Britain's nuclear deterrent, he did not realize that rather than confirming Britain's continuing role as an autonomous international player, he was demonstrating her growing dependence on the US.

The problem was that the Americans had decided to discontinue their support for the Skybolt missile programme, with which they had intended to equip British aircraft. They were now thinking of supplying Polaris missiles, which would create a deeper dependence on US technology than with Skybolt. Macmillan had actually mentioned this possibility at a meeting with de Gaulle at Rambouillet, before leaving for Nassau. But he did not read sufficiently well between the lines of de Gaulle's more general remarks the doubts that de Gaulle increasingly felt about British membership of the Community.

When Macmillan secured from Kennedy a good financial and technical deal for Polaris, which in his view preserved Britain's freedom of action and made the system available through NATO to the French, he thought he had achieved a triumph. For de Gaulle, however, this was confirmation of his long-standing fears about the British. He had no interest in making France dependent on NATO, still less on the Anglo-Saxons. A whispering campaign began in the French press about how this was all but a stage in the US administration's 'Grand Design' to make the EEC part of a wider US sphere of influence, with Britain as its Trojan horse.

While Heath and his team were still negotiating the fine print of agricultural transition arrangements, de Gaulle surprised the world at a press conference in the Elysée Palace on 14 January 1963 with a public rejection of Britain's application. Speaking without a note but with sweeping theatrical gestures, he mixed specific criticism of Britain's nuclear arrangements with generalized doubts about Britain's ability ever to play a wholehearted role in Europe. Representatives of the Five, unconsulted and appalled, did not know what to make of this and talks continued with the British in Brussels in a desultory way for a few days longer. But after the French government made clear that this was indeed a formal veto, the negotiations were wound up by the end of the month.

In the short term, this was followed by consolidation of the EEC in a number of important respects. The Common Agricultural Policy was applied in important sectors such as dairy products, beef and veal, with common prices agreed for cereals. The European Court of Justice was establishing its own authority, based on the doctrine of the supremacy of Community law over national law. At the same time, de Gaulle formalized France's new friendship with the Federal Republic of Germany by signing the Elysée Treaty with Adenauer – within days of rejecting Britain's membership application. The following few years saw a significant thickening up of relations between the political, bureaucratic and industrial élites in the two countries.

But the crunch was coming for de Gaulle's alternative model of how the EEC should function. Having seen the Fouchet proposals foiled, he decided on a trial of strength with the Commission when Hallstein proposed, in early 1965, new arrangements to deal with the growing EEC budget.

He sought to make agricultural levies payable directly to the Community, which meant giving the Commission what became known as 'own resources' for its budgetary priorities; and to include in the oversight arrangements for such funds a degree of majority voting between member states which would be carried through in conjunction with voting in the Parliamentary Assembly. This was in de Gaulle's view the thin end of the wedge in undermining Member States' rights and he used a parallel negotiation on agricultural prices to hold these insitutional proposals hostage. When Hallstein refused to back down, with the support of the Court of Justice, de Gaulle withdrew his representatives and implemented a French 'empty chair' policy for six months – ensuring at the same time that interim agricultural payments were made so that French farmers did not lose out.

A solution came at the beginning of 1966 with the Luxembourg compromise, a 'Gentlemen's Dis-agreement' under which it was recognized that majority voting should not apply when a state believed its vital national interests would be affected by any draft proposal. The Court was not involved in the agreement and the precise status of this essentially political arrangement was not made entirely clear. It contained an admonition that states should do all they could to agree. But it made explicit what Hallstein had concluded in private – that no country's vital interests would ever be outvoted. Coming at a time when Member States were increasingly calling the shots on questions affecting them, notably through the Committee of Permanent Representatives (COREPER) which was meeting weekly in Brussels, the agreement was in line with the times. It has become a crucial, if informal, component of the *acquis communautaire*, the heritage of commitments and obligations passed down within the Community. It was certainly not what Monnet had in mind at this stage.

But it probably made things easier for the Labour government in Britain, which since Gaitskell's time had come round to the same view as its Conservative predecessors on the EEC: that access to the common market and competition with continental producers would give British industry its best chance of breaking the vicious cycle of low productivity, low profits and low investment. Harold Wilson, the Prime Minister, was no great enthususiast and his party remained divided on the issue. But following a grand tour of Community capitals with his more pro-European Foreign Secretary, George Brown, he revived Britain's membership application in July 1967. Wilson had probably read the French as inaccurately as Macmillan before him and provided de Gaulle with a pretext for a veto – rather similar to the Skybolt affair – when he presided over a substantial devaluation of sterling in November that year. Having failed to warn his putative Community partners in advance, he was portrayed as falling into the old British tradition of going it alone. De Gaulle highlighted British economic weakness as one of the main reasons when he cast his second veto, on 27 November.

It is worth mentioning in passing the 'Soames Affair' of February 1969, when President de Gaulle canvassed with the British ambassador, Sir Christopher Soames, the idea of setting up a 'directorate' of the major European powers, France, Britain, the FRG and Italy, to dominate a wider European free trade area. This showed a definite willingness to reverse the direction of integration. Certainly, when France decided to devalue the franc two years after the UK, there was no advance discussion with other EEC members.

But by that time, France had a new President. De Gaulle's forceful leadership, which had provided the platform for powerful economic growth at home and the reassertion of French pride abroad, had generated new problems. The revolt of students and workers in the spring of 1968, for all its vigour, actually strengthened his position in the short term. But it led indirectly to the rejection of his proposals for constitutional reform in a referendum a year later. His replacement that summer by the moderate Gaullist, Georges Pompidou, suddenly opened up new perspectives both for Britain and for the Community itself.

The mechanical process of integration was advancing well, with total abolition of customs duties and achievement of a Common External Tariff earlier than anticipated in July 1968. The impact of the EEC was identified closely with the economic boom in the Member States, in contrast to lower rates of growth across Britain and EFTA. There was nevertheless a lack of coherence in the way the Community was developing. Morale in the Commission was low, Hallstein having been squeezed out for his temerity in standing up to de Gaulle. Pompidou now conjured up a new prospectus at his first major press conference on 10 July 1969, promising *achèvement, approfondissement, élargissement*, 'completion, deepening and enlargement' of the Community. There was still a series of misunderstandings with the Germans, over the Council of Ministers which was due to be the forum for this relaunch, and with other Member States, who feared a repeat of the Fouchet Committee.

But in the event Pompidou showed a clear will to work with his colleagues, notably the new Federal

German Chancellor, Willy Brandt, who took office in October. He called a special summit to take place at The Hague on 1–2 December. The monetary instability of the late 1960s, occasioned by growing US deficits and an abrupt rise in commodity prices, was playing havoc with the weaker currencies in Europe. This in turn put a strain on agricultural prices and arrangements for industrial trade across currency lines. Long standing French interest in this question made monetary union a natural question for the agenda. There was also a revived initiative on political co-operation, though this time the Commission was reassured that it would not be just another attempt to cut back the powers of Brussels. Similarly, the agenda items on agriculture and future enlargement of the EEC were prepared in a way to maximize progress.

The Hague Summit is usually portrayed as marking the second 'relaunch' of the Community. It lived up to its ambitious advance billing. Pompidou led with a strong plea for a plan to be drafted within a year for full monetary union. Ministers were instructed to study prospects for progress on political unification, which led to the appointment of the important Davignon Committee. Upbeat language on the desirability of enlarging the Community, unthinkable a year before, was included, as a clear signal to Britain and the other potential applicants. The Commission at last got its 'own resources'. The impression was of a new will to grip the interconnected problems of currencies, farm prices and barriers to trade, with the Commission and the Member States, and an increasingly vocal European Parliament, working at last on the same side. The declaration said that 'The Community has now arrived at a turning point in its history . . . paving the way for a united Europe capable of assuming its responsibilities in the world of tomorrow and making a contribution commensurate with its traditions and its mission'.

In any decade but the 1970s, this huge prospectus might just have been achievable. But the skies were already darkening. The postwar boom was losing momentum and commodity prices and inflation were rising around the world. Events in the Middle East would have the last word.

FOUR

Enlarging without Deepening: Brussels to Fontainebleau, 1970–84

Edward Heath's belief in Britain's European destiny had two dimensions. Like many in his generation who had served in the war, he saw British participation in Europe's institutions as vital for the long-term security of the continent. But he also believed that playing a full part in a dynamic European economy was the only way of achieving modernization of Britain's archaic industrial structures. Almost uniquely, he had made Europe the subject of his maiden speech in the House of Commons in 1951. With his command of the dossier from the initial negotiations in the 1960s, he was well placed as prime minister to carry the process through. At a critical two-day meeting with President Pompidou in May 1971, he conveyed the forceful

43

impression that Britain was going to be a whole-hearted member of the Community.

Heath's main difficulties were domestic, since his House of Commons majority included a number of Conservatives who rejected the Community and all its works on principles of national sovereignty. The Labour Party moved quickly in opposition to adopt a more critical stance than it had in government and a strong movement developed at the grass roots of the party and trade unions to reject whatever terms Heath's government negotiated. Since the 1960s, some of the edge had been taken out of the Commonwealth debate by changing patterns of trade. But there still had to be special arrangements for Caribbean sugar and New Zealand dairy products. More importantly, it was clear that the financial costs of membership would now be higher, both because of the level of subsidized food prices under the Common Agricultural Policy (CAP) compared with world prices and because of the way that Britain's EEC budget contribution would be calculated – on the basis of its food imports which were proportionately higher than those of its partners.

Nevertheless, the negotiations which were brought to a successful conclusion in Brussels probably gave Britain as good a deal as it could hope for at the time. Heath was supported in most of the important votes in the House of Commons by Roy Jenkins and a large enough number of Labour pro-Europeans to outweigh Conservative opponents. On one division, which Heath won by only eight votes, it was the tiny pro-European Liberal Party which kept him on course. The broad strategy was that although much may be wrong with the prospectus Britain was accepting, it would be best to try and change it from within.

This meant swallowing things which would come back to haunt subsequent governments: an agricultural system which was supporting inefficient continental farmers at high cost to consumers, and a level of British contributions which after an eight-year transition would bite very hard. The Six had also smuggled through a Common Fisheries Policy (CFP) in June 1970, in advance of possible EEC membership not so much of the UK as of Norway, which had also applied to join. The CFP was to raise serious problems for the UK after the end of its transition period.

In the event, the CFP probably tipped the balance in the Norwegian referendum which rejected membership. But the UK's erstwhile EFTA partner, Denmark, joined the EEC with Britain, as did the Republic of Ireland on 1 January 1973. While

Danish membership would always prove controversial at home, Ireland made an unqualified success of its participation in Europe, both in confirming its national identity outside Britain's shadow, and in achieving high levels of economic prosperity, which were supported by EC assistance programmes.

However, the Community they joined was in greater turmoil than had been expected after the warm words of The Hague Declaration. The Werner Committee on monetary union had reported robustly on the need for Economic and Monetary Union (EMU) by 1980 and this aspiration was endorsed at head-of-government level at the Paris Summit in October 1972. But, there had been tensions within Werner's committee between a French attitude, which gave primacy to fixing exchange rates, and the German approach, which was to concentrate on aligning the economies of the Member States. This difference of emphasis was to haunt discussion of EMU for the next twenty years. At this stage, with constant speculative attacks on the franc and continuing pressure to revalue the D-Mark, the circle could not be squared. The turbulence brought to world markets by the oil crisis in October 1973 put paid to any serious prospect of monetary union in the medium term. However, in the way of the Community, lessons were learnt which were to be drawn upon subsequently.

The British were making a sticky start, generally being seen to adopt a negative role in the monetary discussions to which others attached great importance. There was particular resentment that having argued forcefully for the creation of a European Regional Development Fund (ERDF), which her new partners were willing to concede as a way of boosting what Britain got back from the Community, she now seemed unwilling to accept the quid pro quo of at least tacit support for EMU.

The year 1973, acclaimed by Henry Kissinger as the 'Year of Europe', turned out to be a travesty, as even modest and sensible proposals advanced by Commissioner Etienne Davignon to promote co-operation on foreign policy questions were overshadowed in a greater quarrel about how to deal with the US. Whenever they were incapable of summoning up sufficient solidarity to feud on the same side against the Americans, the Member States simply feuded among themselves. When the Yom Kippur War presented a series of challenges combining Middle East politics, economic crisis and financial emergency, the result was unsurprising incoherence from the Community. One significant element in this was the refusal of the British to go along with a Community Energy Policy – which they had supported until it became a practical possibility, at just the time that considerable reserves of oil were discovered under the North Sea.

But the problems went still deeper within the UK. If Heath was operating against a background of miners' strikes and episodic industrial action in the early part of his administration, he found himself utterly embattled in late 1973 and early 1974, facing a complete shutdown of the coal mines and a three-day week for industry. When Harold Wilson and his increasingly anti-European Labour Party returned to power following a general election on 28 February, it was clear that the British membership dossier would have to be re-opened. After a further election consolidated his position the following October, Wilson demanded renegotiation of the terms of the Treaty of Accession.

He was fortunate that there had been a change of the guard elsewhere, with Giscard d'Estaing replacing Georges Pompidou, who died in April 1974, and the pragmatic Helmut Schmidt taking over from Willy Brandt the following month. He met a greater willingness to be lenient with Britain's difficulties than he might have expected, and mounted a shrewd campaign to have key aspects looked at again: the British contribution, CAP reform and a better deal for Commonwealth trading partners. Insofar as negotiations on these questions were continuing in the normal run of Community business, it was possible to present as the substance of renegotiation some things that were happening anyway, notably through the Lome Convention which was preparing a new deal for France's and other Member States' colonies. This was portrayed as improving the deal for Commonwealth countries.

Between progress in setting up the ERDF, a bit of forward accounting on the budget and some creative thinking about how world food prices were now catching up with EEC prices, it was possible to present a package which Community heads of government accepted at the Dublin Summit in March 1975 – this which could plausibly be presented to British opinion as an improvement on what the Conservatives had secured.

Managing this domestic dimension showed Wilson's consummate skill as a political operator. In fact his handling of the issue made a huge and enduring contribution to Britain's relationship with the rest of the Community. There had been a state of open civil war in the Labour Party since the autumn of 1971, with the overwhelming majority of the party's trade union and constituency supporters opposed to Britain's EEC membership. But there was still a majority in favour in Cabinet, if not in Wilson's own immediate circle. As an agnostic himself, who never felt at home with Community affairs, his priority was keeping the Labour Party together. He decided to pick up on the idea of a national referendum – which came from Labour's anti-European Left – as the best prospect both for exorcising the demons in his party and for securing a sustainable policy for the party and for the nation.

Wilson played a less than energetic role in the campaign, even though his government commended to voters the terms they had negotiated. He reluctantly permitted his Home Secretary, Roy Jenkins, to be the leading Labour member of a coalition for a 'Yes' vote, together with senior figures from the other parties. The pro-Europe lobby managed skilfully to send out the right signals in the course of its high-spending campaign, in the face of unenthusiastic public opinion and a generally hostile press. The result of the referendum, on 5 June 1975, was decisive: 67 per cent in favour, which would have been difficult to envisage a year before.[1]

The misfortune was that the membership prospectus was accepted by many voters as something cost-free: even though some campaigners were quite open about the political dimension, the overwhelming impression, especially through the media, was of the likely economic benefits rather than any political costs or obligations. Certainly very little was said about the ambitions or expectations of Britain's Community partners. In the short term this did not make much difference, because Europe was embarking on its wilderness years, a period variously described as the 'locust years' or the years of 'Eurosclerosis'. The 1970s were of course a decade of economic difficulty and adjustment worldwide. But it gradually became clear that the EEC Member States were performing less well in growth and unemployment terms than their main international competitors, the US and Japan. The most significant report of the time, written in 1975 for the European Council by Leo Tindemans, Prime Minister of Belgium, correctly discerned a lack of direction in the Community. But its recommendations suggested contentious supranational powers. Despite the report containing some good ideas for bringing the institutions closer to the people, there was not the political will for it to be acted upon.

But there was one area which the new political leadership in the Community did feel equipped to tackle, and that was monetary co-operation. Giscard d'Estaing and Helmut Schmidt were both economists by background. They had similar thoughts on the need to find new ways of stabilizing the international economy following the collapse of the Bretton Woods System and disruptions brought by an unstable dollar. Their answer was to create a zone of currency stability in Europe. They found support for this approach not only in the work done by the Werner Committee earlier in the decade, but also in the enthusiasm of Commission officials for making monetary union the next arena for pressing integration. There was an added incentive for Schmidt in that German exporters were suffering badly from frequent lurches upwards in the value of the D-Mark.

Jim Callaghan, who succeeded Wilson as British Prime Minister in March 1976, was in contrast to Giscard and Schmidt not keen on monetary union. In bringing the IMF to London that autumn to help bail out the British economy, he predictably favoured a more Anglo-Saxon approach to economic problems. But his old colleague Roy Jenkins, who became President of the European Commission at the beginning of 1977, became convinced of the need for action at a European level and launched the idea of a European Monetary System (EMS) later that year. The proposal that he developed with Giscard and Schmidt was to create a new European Currency Unit (the ECU), based on a basket of European currencies which would be supported by contributions from Member States' reserves; and an Exchange Rate Mechanism (ERM) according to which members would peg their currencies against the ECU with only limited room for fluctuation This was intended to promote stability, exercise downward pressure on inflation and encourage trade within the Community.

In Britain, there was strong resistance – much of it understandable. A lower proportion of British trade took place within Europe and the value of sterling was affected both by the greater amount of trade with the US and by sterling's emerging status as a petro-currency. The Labour Party Conference of October 1978 gave Callaghan such a rocky ride over the EMS that it would have been extremely difficult for him to accept full membership even if he would have liked to. As it was, the Treasury reinforced all his natural prejudices against and the question did not really arise. Nevertheless, the structure agreed made it possible for Britain to become a formal member of the EMS, playing its part in setting up the ECU, without taking on the obligations of membership of the ERM by fixing the value of sterling. This was the course Callaghan adopted when the EMS came into operation in March 1979.

The historically different French and German approaches to economic and monetary union were still not reconciled in the early years of the EMS, and there were subsequently a number of adjustments to the parity of the franc. But the last major change, in March 1983, turned out to be the moment of truth for the French economy. The Finance Minister, Jacques Delors, persuaded the Germans to accept a substantial revaluation of the D-Mark, in tandem with a franc devaluation. But more important, he persuaded his President François Mitterrand to impose a tough austerity package on the French economy. This represented the end of that government's strategy of 'socialism in one country' on the back of an unsustainable exchange rate. It also demonstrated a new attention to economic fundamentals which the Germans could only applaud. The exchange rate thus became not only France's principal macroeconomic indicator, but the symbol of a system which now proved its staying power. The EMS was to play an ever more critical role as monetary union became a serious possibility in the course of the 1980s.

But the political leaders of the EEC had another, even more explosive challenge to deal with after they set up the EMS in 1979. This was Margaret Thatcher, who became British Prime Minister after her election victory in May. Thatcher had seized the leadership of the Conservative Party as an apparently more vigorous alternative to Edward Heath, who was not forgiven for losing two general elections. Mrs

Thatcher criticized Heath for his failure to stick by the more market-driven domestic policies he had originally advocated. However, she did not come into office with a thorough-going radical programme, nor was she perceived as particularly anti-European, having played a highly visible role in the referendum campaign in 1975. But one of her greatest qualities was an extraordinary single-mindedness, supported by a flair for detail and a populist sense of natural justice. When she came to grips with the problem of the British budget contribution to the EEC, she found an issue that could have been designed for her – and she brought to the Community table a negotiating style it had never seen before.

There would have been a budget crisis even if Jim Callaghan had won the election. As the UK's seven-year transitional period after joining ran out, it was clear that the way the CAP and the budget were operating was still very bad for Britain: over two-thirds of EEC spending was on agriculture, from which Britain gained little, while ERDF funding was still on a very modest scale. This meant that although Britain was one of the poorest members of the Community in per capita terms, it was being asked to pay a net contribution of between £800m and one billion pounds a year. This was far more than any other Member State. There had been a political agreement at the time of the Accession Agreement that a solution would be found if an 'unacceptable situation' were to arise. Mrs Thatcher raised the question in moderate terms at her first European Council in Strasbourg the month after she was elected. But when she went to the Dublin Council in November 1979, she was so appalled by the Commission proposal of a mere $350m rebate that she harangued her fellow heads of government with a full-throated demand for 'our money back'. This set the tone for relations with her colleagues for the next five years.

Giscard and Schmidt, still the main players in the Council, were unimpressed. According to many observers they patronized Mrs Thatcher in a way she never forgave. The Dublin Council broke up without any substantive progress, and temporary solutions had to be found to get the budgets through for the next two years. However, an objective Commission study showed that there was considerable justice on the British side. The problem was implementing a satisfactory solution in a way that would be equitable to all of the Member States and would take account of separate, continuing wrangles over agricultural prices and budget reform. Mrs Thatcher was not afraid of vetoing new CAP prices in 1982 unless she received satisfaction. But her opponents had no qualms about outvoting her when majority voting applied – and also in instances when she believed that majority voting did not apply, which just poured further fuel on the flames.

By 1983, she found her leverage greater because the Community was literally running out of money. It needed unanimous authorization from Member States to raise the ceiling on national VAT contributions, from which a large proportion of EC funding was now drawn. But as agreement seemed to loom closer, Mrs Thatcher stuck by her view of fairness. After President Mitterrand made a strong attempt to break the deadlock in March 1984, authorizing an offer from the Commission of one million ecus, against her demand for 1.35 million ecus, Mrs Thatcher famously said 'no', overruling the recommendation of her Foreign Secretary, Lord Carrington.

An alternative formula was worked out in time for the Fontainebleau Council in June, which had the effect of giving her one million ecus for 1984 and an arrangement for future years that she found acceptable: this was defined as being an 'abatement' of Britain's contribution equal to 66 per cent of the difference between her VAT contributions to the budget and what came back by way of Community programmes. Although some critics say even today that the Mitterrand offer she had rejected was actually a better deal for Britain, the new formula did the trick in defusing the EC's financial crisis. It had the effect of making Germany by far the largest net contributor and, with time, Britain was overtaken in net contributions per head by the Dutch as well.

Fontainebleau was an important Council in other ways. As well as bringing the long-running budget saga to a close, with a clearer definition of the Community's 'own resources', it established what would become an important committee under an Irish Senator, James Dooge, to consider the way forward for the Community. A second body, the Committee for a People's Europe, was set up under an Italian chairman, Pietro Adonnino, and this did important work on questions of European citizenship and identity. The British also presented their own paper, 'Europe – The Future', which argued for a new push towards freeing up the Community's internal market.

The EC was coming of age. On the foreign policy front, there was now a network of 'expert groups' co-ordinated by a political committee of senior officials in Brussels, and a growing habit of effective co-ordination in international organizations. The Venice Declaration on the Middle East in 1980 had shown that Member States were not afraid of taking a different view from the US on a major international question. And at the time of the Falklands War, the British had been mildly surprised at the support they received from their partners on the basis of Community solidarity. The Europeans also worked well together in opposing Ronald Reagan's sanctions on economic co-operation with the Soviet Union. The Greeks had joined the Community in 1981, which had an important role both in securing democracy and ensuring a Western orientation in that country. The Portuguese and the Spanish were negotiating their way in, sure in the knowledge that EC membership would anchor their still fragile democracies as well. So there seemed to be reasons for optimism, maybe more than at The Hague fourteen years before.

But nothing had prepared the British – or anyone else – for the pace of events that was to confront the Community over the rest of the decade.

FIVE

Forcing the Pace: Milan to Rome (again), 1985–90

In January 1985, the European Commission took delivery of the most driven and determined leader in its history. Jacques Delors arrived with the reputation of a steely finance minister who had managed against the odds to drag the French socialist party into recognizing the harsh realities of modern economics. His unflattering image was that of a colourless technocrat.

He was more complicated, more rich in contradictions. than either of these stereotypes. A devout Christian Socialist, he was by turns emotional and philosophical, bullying then solicitous. His exceptional gifts were command of ideas and ruthlessness in turning them into facts on the ground. He approached the office of President of the Commission in a more purposive way than his predecessors, setting up an elaborate network of people across the

Directorates who saw their prime responsibility as being to him and his private office, his *cabinet*. In dealing with heads of government and foreign ministers, he would play up the importance of his office one minute in a haughty and even offensive manner and then apply himself to establishing a personal, even intimate rapport with those who would matter most to him. He committed serious tactical errors and made many enemies. But no one ever doubted the boldness of his thinking or his willingness to take risks to make things happen.

The Europe he confronted was beginning to emerge from the 'Eurosclerosis' of the late 1970s and early '80s. The economies of Western Europe had suffered their first period of prolonged stagnation in the postwar period, especially in comparison with the US and the 'tiger economies' of the Far East. Delors decided to exploit the improving economic environment by playing up the idea of the European Single Market and the huge gains each of the Member States would make by dismantling the economic barriers which still remained between them almost thirty years after the start of the EEC. The encouragement of trade within the Community had always been at the heart of Monnet's thinking. Delors saw scope for a quantum leap.

The ground had been well prepared in a series of reports, from the very grand Solemn Declaration of European Unity in Stuttgart in June 1983 to the Dooge Report[1] which was now emerging under the mandate of the Fontainebleau Summit. There was also a strong head of steam behind the single market idea in the European Parliament, spearheaded by a group of MEPs including the Italian communist, Altiero Spinelli, and the British industrialist, Basil de Ferranti. They were known as the Kangaroo Group after the Strasbourg restaurant in which they used to meet. Strasbourg was emerging as something of a second EC capital. However, as long as MEPs held as many of their meetings as they could in Brussels, it could not really compete. But MEPs were effective in making the Single Market one of 'their' causes. The story of European union is, of course, peppered with declarations, aspirations and ginger groups: it was Delors' skill to draw on all of these internal market initiatives for his own purpose, which was re-launching the process of integration.

Delors could assume that the British would come along helpfully, since Mrs Thatcher had made clear that the internal market was a priority for her. His special stroke of genius was to entrust the task of making it happen to Mrs Thatcher's newly appointed Conservative Commissioner, Lord Cockfield, who came from being her Minister of Trade. He had also been Chief Executive of Boots the Chemists and was well on top of the practical aspects of the dossier.

The legal and philosophical basis for the Single Market initiative actually went back to well before Stuttgart and Fontainebleau, when the European Court in Luxembourg ruled in the famous 'Cassis de Dijon' case in 1979. A West German food importer had been prevented from importing this famous blackcurrant spirit on the basis that it had too low an alcohol content to be classed as a liqueur but was too strong to be classified as wine. The European Court determined that the West German authorities were practising unjustifiable protectionism in excluding the foreign import. They went on to establish the principle that manufacturers should be able to sell their products as readily in other national markets of the EC as in their own – subject to a number of health, safety and environmental factors that are spelled out in the Treaty of Rome.

The implication of this ruling was that the myriad of petty regulations, obstructions and informal practices protecting local producers around Europe were now open to challenge. Business people around the EC saw huge scope for exporting their products into markets which they had found difficult to crack, from car assembly to agricultural produce and government procurement programmes. Delors' cabinet worked very closely with Lord Cockfield as he put together a White Paper listing some 280 measures to be taken, with a hard deadline of the end of 1992 for implementation. The precision of the timetable was one of the most striking successes of the programme: not only was it just about achievable, exerting the maximum pressure on governments to deliver once they had signed up. It was also something that ordinary people could understand, whether as entrepreneurs, workers or consumers. As the message came across through some polished public relations work that the '1992 programme' would increase choice and thereby enhance wealth, the EC achieved something quite rare in its history: a genuinely popular campaign which made promises on which the Community was able to deliver.

In the event there were some areas from the initial list where it proved impossible to create a genuine free market, while the Cecchini Report of 1986–8 revealed new ones beyond the White Paper where progress could be made. By the end of 1992 it was recognized that 'completing' the Single Market was rather like painting the Forth Bridge – as soon as the job was finished it would be necessary to start over again, as new technologies took over and businesses and governments found new ways around the rules. But hardly anyone would now deny that the programme was a success. Many years on there are still arguments involving supporters of the Commission and of the Parliament, of Jacques Delors and of Margaret Thatcher, about who really had the idea in the first place.

For the integrationists such as Delors, the Single Market was simply the first stage in a broader assault. The Stuttgart Declaration had been followed by a draft Treaty on European Union from the European Parliament, proposing initiatives across a range of areas including monetary union, social provision and changes to the institutional framework of the EC. These were picked up forcefully in the Dooge Committee recommendations when they emerged in final form in March 1985. The integrationists saw correctly that there would have to be changes to the Treaty of Rome to entrench the Single Market legislation and this would require an Inter-Governmental Conference (IGC). That would in turn provide the opportunity to achieve progress in other fields. President Mitterrand and Chancellor Kohl were beginning to practise their own version of the 'highest common multiple' approach in framing joint Franco-German proposals before European Councils. They could usually rely on the Italians and the Benelux countries – the other members of the original Six – to back them. Given the energetic performance of Delors, this amounted to a formidable coalition for change, against the more disparate group of doubters consisting of the UK, Denmark and Greece.

It was the Milan Summit of June 1985 which set the agenda for the next phase of integration. The British did not come without a plan, indeed their proposals for achieving better co-ordination on foreign policy questions were probably better thought through than the competing Franco-German draft. But as far as the politics was concerned, there was a majority vote against the British, the Danes and the Greeks in calling an IGC to discuss the broader treaty changes which would be necessary – with the final sting in the tail of a reference to economic and monetary union which Mrs Thatcher felt had been slipped in behind her back. There was something in this – but the reality was that the integrationists already had the votes if they cared to deploy them on anything relating to the principle of holding an IGC. Her last resort would be the veto, to which she was entitled, on any changes to the treaty which she believed would undermine the UK's national interest. In practice, she believed the need for that was still some way off.

The IGC process went ahead briskly, with intensive, behind-the-scenes consultations punctuated by major meetings in Brussels and Luxembourg from September to December 1985. Delors and the Commission played a subordinate role, with the French, the Germans and the British playing out most of the conflicts, especially on the foreign policy questions underlying European Political Co-operation (EPC). The upshot was two treaties, one on EPC and one on the array of changes affecting the EEC of which the centrepiece was the Single Market programme. The two sets of proposals were brought together, under an inspired idea from Delors, as the Single European Act, to confer coherence on what was a ragbag of politically disparate issues.

The legacy was in the event more compelling than might have been expected at the time. The act is often praised in retrospect for the clarity and precision of its drafting, which compares well with the treaties of Rome and Maastricht. Its rhetoric is consistent, stressing at every turn the act's intention of promoting 'concrete progress towards European unity'. But it is moderate in tone, promising modestly for instance to adopt measures 'with the aim of progressively establishing the internal market'.

The act made the distinction between the Communities 'operating in accordance with their own rules' on trade and economic questions, and the sphere of EPC which preserved an intergovernmental framework. But it contained a number of institutional innovations, most critically the extended use of majority voting. Mrs Thatcher had acknowledged this as necessary to prevent Member States exploiting the principle of unanimity to protect their sectional interests against the justified claims of the Single Market – she had the Greeks particularly in mind. This was to come back to haunt her, as was the brief chapter[2] of the Single Act whose title was Co-operation in Economic and Monetary Policy.

As so often in the history of the EU, the British would now have been content with a period of consolidation, allowing the new provisions on political co-operation to take effect. But even before the Single Act came into force on 1 July 1987, the integrationists were arguing the case that there could be no true single market without a single currency. Otherwise countries would seek unfair competitive advantage against each other through devaluation. The dismantling of capital controls, under the Single Market programme, would also increase the scope for speculators to attack individual currencies.

The Italian economist, Tomasso Padoa-Schioppa, had already written a report earlier that year setting out this analysis for the Commission. A further boost to this sort of thinking came when Wall Street crashed in October, amid international squabbling about interest rates and currency parities. The French Finance Minister, Balladur, argued in a memorandum to EC Finance Ministers that the growing risks of currency instability required more than a tightening up of the ERM. A European Central Bank was the answer. As the French pressed the Germans along traditional lines, the case for movement was also made in a joint article by the two old stagers of the monetary scene, both now out of office – Giscard d'Estaing and Helmut Schmidt.

Governments of Member States had in the meantime been scrapping about the budget again. Delors led from the front in trying to get a mechanism agreed to put a ceiling on CAP expenditure and provide a framework for the future. At the cost of a row with the British, a threat to resign and a commitment to provide funding to the poorer Mediterranean countries, known as Club Med and led by the Spaniards who were now full EC members, a deal was done on the 'Delors Package': this set a clear limit on growth of the EC budget so that it would rise by 1992 to a ceiling fixed at 1.2 per cent of total GNP of the Community.

Emboldened by his success, Delors went to the Hanover Council of June 1987 with the Padoa-Schioppa report under his arm and a set of fresh ideas for relaunching EMU. He benefited from his 'second honeymoon', attendant on the adoption of the budget package and successful ratification of the Single European Act, to be renominated as President of the Commission – with Mrs Thatcher among his sponsors. But no sooner was he confirmed in office than he got himself appointed to preside over a Committee of the Member States' Central Bank Governors, with a mandate to recommend on the progressive realization of EMU as set out in the Single Act. Some sort of committee was inevitably going to be set up, in particular to discuss the implications of the abolition of exchange controls. The remarkable thing was that Delors was put in charge, through a combination of personal *chutzpah*, support from President Mitterrand, and misjudgement by the Germans of what they were committing themselves to.

Chancellor Kohl was at this time no EMU-enthusiast. The President of the Bundesbank, Karl-

Otto Pöhl, was an outright opponent. They doubted that much would come of the Delors Committee. The British saw it as a good way of kicking the ball off into the long grass, since the Governor of the Bank of England, Robin Leigh-Pemberton, also no fan of EMU, was a member. But rather like the target date of 1992, the act of setting a deadline – that the committee should report back to the Madrid Council in June 1989 – had the effect of concentrating minds.

Delors showed enormous intellectual agility and personal charm in cajoling twelve bankers into considering not so much the principle of whether a European Central Bank was a good thing as how it could be made to work if a political decision were taken in favour. During the meetings in Basle between September 1988 and April 1989, Delors leaned heavily on Padoa-Schioppa, whom he had brought into the Committee as joint *rapporteur*. Together, they developed a model which would finesse the traditional difference between the French approach, concentrating on the monetary side, and the German, which put economic fundamentals first. Delors orchestrated, and sometimes even ventriloquized, the views of the Governors so well that when the draft report was adopted by the Committee, both Pöhl and Leigh Pemberton felt able to sign up.

The outlines of the EMU proposal put by the Delors Committee, as they emerged in April 1989, were not far removed from the provisions that ultimately went into the Maastricht Treaty at the end of 1991. The model for the European Central Bank (ECB) was the German Bundesbank, the banker's central bank, with its towering reputation for rigour and independence from political pressure. The ECB's governors would be nominated by national governments. But in issuing and controlling the new single currency which would replace national currencies, their priorities would be those of the ECB itself rather than those of the Member States or of other European Community institutions. A further, crucial innovation to emerge from the Delors Committee was the idea of 'convergence criteria' which Member States would have to satisfy in order to qualify for inclusion in EMU: a set of 'good housekeeping' rules to do with levels of borrowing, inflation and debt to indicate whether they were running their economies prudently enough to be a benefit rather than a liability to the other members.

But discussion of EMU was not going on in a political vacuum. Mrs Thatcher's honeymoon with Jacques Delors did not long survive his re-appointment. She did not like the way he handled

either the budget negotiation or EMU. She mis-
trusted his championing of a Social Charter for
workers, which reflected his Christian Socialist belief
that the individualism being promoted in the work on
the Single Market should be balanced by attention to
workers' collective rights. Delors had no interest in a
bosses' Europe. Going with the grain of what is called
'social policy' in most continental countries, Delors
presented a set of ideas, at a trades union conference
in Stockholm in May 1988, which stressed the need to
lay down minimum standards for working conditions.
He compounded the sin in Mrs Thatcher's eyes by
appearing at the British Trades Union Congress the
following September, making a forceful case for the
gains which Britain's trade unionists would reap if
they could overcome their instinctive anti-
Europeanism to play a more constructive role in
Europe. The conference hall resounded to a cheerful
rendition of 'Frère Jacques' in reply.

Mrs Thatcher's riposte came at the College of
Europe in Bruges, on 20 September 1988. In a rich
and robust rejection of the 'corporate' model of
Europe, she stated in ringing tones that: 'We have
not successfully rolled back the frontiers of the State
in Britain only to see them re-imposed at a European
level with a European super-state exercising a new
dominance from Brussels.'

Her attack on the integrated Europe she saw taking shape went further. She described her guiding principle for the EC as willing and active co-operation between independent sovereign states. To try to suppress nationhood and concentrate power at the centre of a 'European conglomerate' would be highly damaging. It would be folly to try and fit the nations of Europe into 'some sort of identikit European personality'.

With these words Mrs Thatcher established a critique which would be taken up initially by the 'Bruges Group' in Britain and subsequently by 'Eurosceptics' on the continent as well. Much of her speech actually sat well with the way a more liberal, market-driven community was now developing thanks to the Single Market. Her exhortation to fellow European leaders to look outward to ensure the prosperity and security of their citizens was entirely in line with the more positive, pragmatic policy which British ministers had now been adopting for some time. And it would be no exaggeration to say that the stress she laid upon the eastern part of the continent was visionary: 'We shall always look on Warsaw, Prague and Budapest as great European cities', she said, well before the collapse of the Warsaw Pact could be taken for granted.

Nevertheless, the legacy of her speech was sourness in the debate and a general feeling that her goals were indeed different from those of other European leaders. When the Madrid Summit of June 1989 determined that the first stage of EMU would start on 1 July 1990, Mrs Thatcher seemed to enter into the spirit by announcing that Britain would join the ERM when certain conditions had been satisfied. It emerged later that she had done this only in response to a joint threat to resign by her Foreign Secretary, Sir Geoffrey Howe, and her Chancellor, Nigel Lawson.

Delors made his intellectual response to Mrs Thatcher in a comprehensive and emotional speech at the College of Brussels almost exactly a year after her own, in October 1989. He announced: 'History is accelerating. So must we . . .'. Politically, he was improving his relationship with Chancellor Kohl and the Germans through his robust support for German unification: events to the East were now working against Mrs Thatcher, whose mixed feelings about the fall of the Berlin Wall made her look as if she was indeed being left behind by history. She was not the only one. François Mitterrand also despaired initially of what a bigger Germany would do to the continental balance of power and he canvassed a series of utterly unsuccessful proposals for a wider

European confederation. But as so often in European affairs, the French were more adept than the British in turning events to their advantage.

In November, John Major replaced Nigel Lawson as Chancellor of the Exchequer following Lawson's tempestuous falling out with Mrs Thatcher. Major canvassed a plan for 'competing currencies' to give the new European currency the chance to prove itself against the existing ones. This could have been a helpful and constructive idea at an earlier stage of the debate. But it was dismissed as a spoiling tactic now. At a summit in Strasbourg on 8 December, the French and the Germans rose above their mutual mistrust over unification by agreeing that an IGC on EMU should take place before the end of 1990. This was the first sign of an implicit deal that if Mitterrand did not obstruct Germany's political unity, then Kohl would accept the principle of EMU which the French favoured – despite a continuing rearguard action against EMU within the Bundesbank.

But there was another part of the quid pro quo. Kohl had made much of the fact that the common German home would be built under a common European roof. He wanted a leap forward towards European political union which he thought would make EMU more saleable within Germany. On 18 April 1990, he and Mitterrand produced another joint Franco-German initiative, calling for reinforcement of the political legitimacy and coherence of the EC. Between two summits in Dublin the momentum grew, and the British found themselves in the familiar position of watching the highest common multiple effect once more. The French and the Germans did another deal in which each of the two sides got the thing they really wanted in exchange for tolerating the thing they did not want – while the British had to digest two things they disliked. A nice irony was that Delors himself was not sure it made sense to go for EMU and political union at the same time. But the political drivers were now taking over. German unity was accomplished in October. The politicians wanted to show they were up to the historic moment.

It fell to Giulio Andreotti, the Italian Prime Minister who chaired the Rome Summit later that month, to drive through the commitment to start the next phase of EMU in 1994. Mrs Thatcher felt betrayed and misused, much as she had in Milan four years earlier, but the writing had been on the wall throughout the political consultations leading up to the Council. She reported back to the House of Commons in such hostile and intemperate terms that Geoffrey Howe, her Deputy Prime Minister since she had ejected him from the Foreign Office, decided to resign from the government. It is a common misapprehension that Mrs Thatcher made her celebrated 'No, No, No' speech in relation to the agreement to move on EMU. Not so. This was in fact her unscripted response to some rather over-the-top remarks to the press from Delors on how political union might work. But only the mood music mattered now. Mrs Thatcher had alienated many of her Cabinet colleagues and backbenchers over Europe and many more of them over domestic questions, notably the poll tax to finance local spending. Howe set in train an irresistible process which culminated in Michael Heseltine's challenge to Mrs Thatcher's leadership, her resignation soon afterwards, and her replacement by John Major.

When a second Rome Summit on 14–15 December launched the IGC on EMU and set guidelines for a political IGC in 1991 the way might have seemed clear for a kinder and gentler discussion of Europe's future. But the removal of Mrs Thatcher was not going to make the path either to EMU, or to political union, a smooth one. Europe's leaders – just about all of them – were riding for a very big fall.

SIX

Triumph and Disaster: Maastricht to Amsterdam – and Beyond, 1991–8

The second Rome Council at the end of 1990 was a more petulant affair than anticipated, a dreary start along the road which would lead to Maastricht. There were Franco-German tensions on EMU, with the Bundesbank hoping it might yet torpedo the whole idea. British ideas on slowing the pace of monetary union won unexpected praise from the Spanish and the Dutch, precipitating an unexpectedly virulent attack on John Major from Jacques Delors. As to the discussions on political union, a Kohl-Mitterrand declaration on 7 December had floated some rather disparate elements for the IGC: reinforcing the European Parliament, beefing up the common foreign and security policy, and converting the Western European Union into the defence agency of the EC. These ran into early opposition from the British, but nevertheless set some sort of agenda for the year ahead. Governments set out on the weary intergovernmental routine of working groups, shuttling between Brussels, Luxembourg and the presidency capitals, negotiating endless proposals, texts and illustrative drafts known splendidly as 'non-papers'.

The Europe of Monnet had been an élitist construction. There had been a certain logic in battle-scarred political leaders clambering from the ruins of war to make historic compromises behind closed doors, and then carrying their parliaments and peoples along with them. This approach had characterized the relations both within and between Member States, and between governments and the Commission – with the exception of the referendums on membership held by the late arrivals, notably the UK, Ireland and Denmark. The routine worked particularly well for the Single Act, on which only the Danes held any serious national debate. However, the disadvantage of this approach was that if the political constituency for integration was not solid, or if popular feeling was not sufficiently taken into account, there would be question marks over the whole enterprise when the going got rough. That was what happened over the immensely complicated but politically explosive contents of the Treaty of Maastricht.

The negotiating process followed a familar pattern. On the political side, the vague guidance from Rome led to a skilfully balanced 'non-paper' from the Luxembourg Presidency. This ignored a more integrationist text from Delors and the Commission, but was vigorously attacked both for being too weak – by the Germans and the Italians, the Belgians and the Dutch, the Spanish, the Portuguese and the Greeks – and for being too strong – by the British and the Danes. This was followed by a second Luxembourg draft, thought to be better – but then scrapped by the incoming Netherlands Presidency, whose gallant attempt to produce a more coherent vision was rejected even more comprehensively in September. The Dutch tabled a further text based on the earlier Luxembourg draft. And so it went on. The political IGC suffered from a lack of the serious preparatory work that had gone into the Single Act – a body like the Dooge Committee would have been helpful in working out what would be attainable.

Behind the impenetrable jargon of the political negotiations, the subject matter of what they were discussing was actually fascinating and urgent. In 1991 there was the Gulf War, followed in the summer by the collapse of Yugoslavia and the unsuccessful coup against President Gorbachev in Moscow. Almost everyone wanted to see the EC making a more robust contribution to international affairs. At the same time, the impact of revolution in Central and Eastern Europe was being felt in the West, particularly through the inflow of between one and two million asylum seekers and other migrants, legal and illegal. For the Germans, the questions arising in terms of refugee, crime and visa policy, were rapidly becoming issues of domestic concern rather than foreign affairs. They wanted a common European response to what became known as the Home Affairs and Justice agenda, and were supported in this by the smaller Member States.

For their part, the British and the French were unwilling simply to extend the competence of the EC to such sensitive areas as foreign policy or home affairs. But they accepted the need for Member States to work more closely together. It was the French Ambassador in Brussels, Boissieu, who came up with the ingenious idea that the 'architecture' of the EC required special 'pillars' to carry policy in these areas, rather than the more organic 'tree' of Community competence, which would have involved majority voting, a central role for the Commission and oversight by the European Parliament. Delors and the integrationists disliked the illogical structure which would result from constructing 'pillars' around the 'tree'. But as Maastricht loomed up before them at the end of the year, the pragmatists who favoured the 'pillars' seemed to be in the ascendant. A joint British/Italian initiative on security policy, agreed between Foreign Ministers Hurd and De Michelis, exposed the limitations on what Member States were really willing to leave to Brussels.

The IGC on EMU was making easier progress, basing itself very clearly on the Delors Report. The 'convergence criteria' were refined to exclude any central control of Member States' taxation policies. But it was agreed at German insistence that they would be applied in such a way that heavy fines would be imposed on governments which lost control of spending. A European Monetary Institute would be set up in 1994 as the precursor of the European Central Bank. The British insisted on being given an 'opt-out' as the price for letting the others proceed with EMU; but they failed in their attempt at the Scheveningen Summit of finance ministers on 1–4 December to make this opt-out available to others. Delors declared in ringing tones that a generalized opt-out would hang over EMU 'like a sword of Damocles' – fearing that the

Germans might just have second thoughts at the last minute. The finance ministers agreed with him and the British got a specific protocol – as did the Danes when they too got cold feet.

The Germans still claimed they needed further progress on political union to counterbalance what they had given on EMU. The principal way of doing this was to enhance the powers of the European Parliament: it was proposed to give the Parliament both a broader remit, taking in new competences such as education, culture, health and the environment, and to create a new form of decision making called co-decision, increasing the Parliament's powers against Commission and Council of Ministers.

When heads of government and their foreign and finance ministers met at Maastricht in the Netherlands on 9–10 December, there was still scope for high drama and emotional, eleventh-hour compromises. Mitterrand and Andreotti bounced their partners into a firm commitment to launch the Single Currency in 1999 if they missed the first target date of 1997. John Major got his terminological pound of flesh by purging from the treaty all mention of 'federalism': this followed a nagging dispute which had rumbled through most of the Luxembourg and Netherlands drafts on including a reference to the 'federal goal' of the European process.[1]

The area of most vigorous debate in the final stages of the summit was the proposed 'Social Chapter' of Maastricht, the lineal descendant of Delors' Social Charter. Britain's Conservative government had consistently kept its distance from the social dimension and all its works. They believed any attempt to assure minimum rights at the workplace would undermine their strategy of achieving competitiveness through flexibility – by encouraging lower wages, part-time working and a lesser degree of job security, on the US model. In response to British concerns, the Dutch Presidency offered to go a long way in watering down the draft text, so that it would have more symbolic than practical effect at the workplace.

But John Major insisted, following a final telephone call to his hard-line Employment Secretary, Michael Howard, that Britain could not negotiate. This led to an ingenious compromise, dreamt up by Delors' *chef de cabinet*, Pascal Lamy, under which Member States were permitted to opt in to a Social Chapter which was not part of the Treaty of Maastricht, but a protocol to it. The Chapter would be implemented using EC machinery and be financed by the Member States including Britain. It would only be integrated properly into the working of the Community in the event of a change of position by the British, who still had the right to veto its inclusion in the Treaty.

There were a number of sub-themes on the way to agreement, which were to assume greater import-ance in the aftermath of Maastricht. One was a change of name: the European Community was henceforth to be subsumed into a European Union, including the CFSP and Home Affairs 'pillars'. The European Community component, the 'tree' in the jargon, continued at the heart of the EU, embody-ing the international legal personality of the Brussels institutions. But the idea that the EC had become a Union, with such a thing as Citizenship of the Union under the new Article 8, was a huge step forward in defining European identity – and this would come back to haunt the originators.

Similarly, an important definition of the arcane concept of 'subsidiarity' appeared in the Treaty, saying that the Community should only take an action when its desired goal could not be achieved sufficiently at the level of the Member States. This was an entirely sensible reassurance that unwarranted intrusion by Brussels into areas of national life would be forbidden under the treaty. But it would be devilishly hard to define in legal terms what con-stituted intrusion, and what was warranted and what was not.

As to the final provisions to be agreed, there was a significant deal on Community 'cohesion', under which large financial transfers were to be made from the rich 'North' to the poorer 'South', to help the latter to meet the demands of EMU. Prime Minister Gonzalez of Spain won a powerful protocol to benefit Spain, Portugal, Greece and Ireland. On the Common Foreign and Security Policy, provision was made for joint actions and common positions going well beyond earlier forms of European Political Co-operation. On Home Affairs and Justice, similar arrangements were made on an intergovernmental basis. John Major fought a late rearguard action in limiting the expansion of the European Parliament's powers, at one stage reducing Chancellor Kohl to exasperation with his tenacity on the question of EC joint research projects.

But the greater legacy was that Chancellor Kohl was now in harness as Europe's power broker. By accepting EMU, he had put Germany and the Bundesbank in pole position. On political union, he had accepted less than his original demands, but he was in a strong position to drive the agenda towards the 1996 Maastricht Review conference which was written into the treaty. And in a subtle, implicit deal in the margins with the British, Kohl had agreed to play a constructive role on the Social Chapter in exchange for British acquiescence in recognition by Member States of the independent governments in Slovenia and Croatia which had emerged from the collapsing Yugoslavia.

This was a complicated story which was not part of the Maastricht agenda. But while diplomats were arguing the wording of a modest improvement in European co-ordination on CFSP, their diplomacy on the ground in the Balkans was failing. President Slobodan Milosevic had defied world opinion in his attacks on Slovenia and Croatia, as the former republics sought to break away from Yugoslavia. The EC had scored some modest early successes in brokering agreements between Milosevic and his Slovene and Croation counterparts; but their diplomacy had subsequently been powerless to prevent Milosevic's Serb militias taking over areas of Croatia with Serb majorities, and sometimes minorities, in a bloody military campaign. It looked as if this might be followed by something even worse in Bosnia, where the population was split between Serbs, Croats and Muslims.

The German position, heavily influenced by domestic opinion including a large Croat community, was strongly in favour of recognizing the embattled Croatia of President Franjo Tudjman. The more cautious British and French position was that this could precipitate civil war among the Bosnians. In reality, the die was probably cast for Bosnia, already brutally polarized between its communities. But there was little honour in the way the British and the French, followed by the other Member States, came round to accepting the German view. The Member States moved to conditional recognition of Croatia on 15 January and under the complex formula agreed, they went on to recognize Bosnia following its independence referendum three months later – an action which precipitated, even if it did not actually cause, the war there.

The EC's diplomatic failure in ex-Yugoslavia had important effects. It showed that even the most integrationist countries like Germany would follow their own national agendas when it suited them – and Germany itself was no longer afraid to bring its weight to bear. When Britain and France went on to commit troops to humanitarian and peacekeeping duties in Bosnia under a UN flag, it was clear that 'Europe', in the shape of the EU, was powerless in its own back yard. This perception paved the way for the US engagement, followed by the NATO operations which belatedly gripped the problem of Bosnia some four years later. Following a singularly unfortunate remark in Croatia by the Luxembourg Foreign Minister in summer 1991 that 'This is the hour of Europe', the legacy was of pessimism and even shame at the Community's failure. This would have the effect of emboldening those who believed the EU should have a stronger mandate in foreign affairs; and also of encouraging those who thought such matters should be left to the Member States, working with NATO and the Americans where this could be effective.

While Sarajevo burned, the immediate challenge to Maastricht came in Copenhagen. The referendum in Denmark, which rejected the treaty on 2 June 1992 by fewer than 50,000 votes, brought together many disparate strands: a long standing Danish belief that power belonged only in the national parliament, the *Folketing*; a resentment of much larger neighbours, particularly Germany; and concern that the high levels of social provision from Denmark's welfare state would somehow be jeopardized. In fact, the Danish result crystallized something much more significant across Europe: the feeling that ordinary people were being taken for granted and that élites of politicians and bureaucrats had, in their enthusiasm for European integration, run far ahead of those whose interests they represented – perhaps even taken the wrong track.

The response in the European Commission was instructive: barely keeping such comments off the record, officials poured contempt upon the Danes, saying they must get their act together fast or get out of the Community. The reaction in Britain, which took on the Presidency in July, was altogether different. Within John Major's Conservative Party and the popular press which until now had broadly supported him, there was a chain reaction which transformed the discussion of Europe. The idea of a small and plucky people having the courage to say 'No' struck a chord. It was taken up together with a number of themes which differed in their emphasis from those in Denmark: the growing interference by Brussels on the basis of Single Market legislation;[2] the threat to economic recovery posed by EC employment laws; and the undermining of British identity and citizenship through the creation of the European Union.

A further strand was resentment of the European Commission and its president, Jacques Delors. The Commission only employed some 15,000 people and real political authority continued to lie with the European Council and its institutions, which were under political control. But there was, nevertheless, a strong impression that unaccountable bureaucrats held great power and were exercising it with arrogance. The British government proceeded cautiously. It said it would find a way of getting the

Danes on board, but disappointed its EC partners in saying that Britain would only ratify Maastricht after this had been achieved. A long-running negotiation to work out special arrangements for the Danes got under way, with the Danish Foreign Minister, Uffe Elleman-Jensen, enunciating the brilliant, neo-Shakespearian sound-bite: 'To be *and* not to be; that is the answer.'

The answer from an Irish referendum on Maastricht on 18 June was less equivocal: 67 per cent in favour. But when François Mitterrand called a similar referendum with a view to reinforcing his domestic position, this backfired dramatically. A powerful opposition coalition was created, including not only obvious opponents like Communists and the National Front, but skilled mainstream politicians of right and left such as Philippe Séguin and Jean-Pierre Chevènement. The uniting factor was not only suspicion of Brussels but uneasiness about the effects of economic modernization, which was identified with the EC and its single market. This was a revolt by those who saw themselves as the losers from 'globalization' of the international economy: farmers, industrial workers and artisans. A further component was rejection of free trade: just the opposite position to the growing anti-Maastricht campaign in Britain. This fierce backlash came within an ace of defeating Maastricht in the referendum on 20 September, winning 48.95 per cent of the vote against 51.05 per cent for the treaty. The result was huge relief for the treaty's supporters around Europe, since without France, Maastricht would have been dead in the water.

But by then, pro-Europeans had suffered another hammer-blow. The financial crisis culminating in 'Black Wednesday' on 16 September knocked Italy out of the ERM and imposed devaluation on Spain, reducing their chances of qualifying for EMU. But the real victim of the ructions in European financial markets, stemming from the Bundesbank policy of using high interest rates to pay for Germany's unification, was Britain.

John Major's Chancellor, Norman Lamont, had used ERM membership as the central plank of his anti-inflation strategy, as Major himself had done as Chancellor before him. The rate at which Britain had joined the ERM was almost certainly too high. When Lamont failed to get the revaluation of the Deutschmark that would have enabled Britain and the others to stay in the system, the pound's fall was dramatic.

But the economic and political effects were contradictory. The low parity for the pound turned out to be the launchpad for a striking export-led recovery in the British economy, which until then had been in deep recession. It could be that the upturn was in any case about to happen. But that is something we shall never know. With no sterling level to defend, it was possible to make substantial cuts in interest rates, and impressive levels of growth were notched up through a prolonged cycle of seven to eight years, seen by some as something of a modern British economic miracle.

Politically, Black Wednesday knocked the stuffing out of the small business people who had been the pro-European core of the Conservative Party. Having carried the pain of what was now seen as an unrealistically high exchange rate, they relished the success which they now identified with their 'escape' from the ERM. Assailed by a powerful campaign from trenchant Eurosceptic journalists, backed by strongly Eurosceptic proprietors such as Rupert Murdoch and Conrad Black, the British commitment to Maastricht began to look wobbly.

This did not prevent a rather skilful British Presidency from rescuing Denmark. First the British held a meeting in Birmingham in October, stressing the importance of subsidiarity and the need for greater transparency in EC procedures as ways of reassuring the Danes. At the Edinburgh Summit in December, they mixed a cocktail almost as rich and complicated as Maastricht itself, providing further reassurance on subsidiarity, rewriting a series of protocols for the Danes including EMU, and agreeing vital provisions on future financing taking in the cohesion funds as well as a budget package to go up to the end of the decade, 'Delors 2'.

The arrangements for Denmark were sufficient to secure a majority of 56 per cent when the second referendum was held on 18 May 1993. But by then the British were centre stage. John Major had won his House of Commons 'paving vote' on Maastricht, after Black Wednesday, by just three votes, as disgruntled Conservatives voted with a Labour Party which was now in favour of Maastricht, but rejected Britain's opt-out from the Social Chapter. The following July, after a further shift in press and public opinion away from Maastricht, more Conservative rebels joined Labour in a motion to adopt the Social Chapter, and this was carried against the government by eight votes. It was only when John Major made the adoption of Maastricht a confidence vote, threatening his party with a general election which they would surely lose, that he won his majority and British ratification was assured.

Elsewhere, ratification was not seriously threatened, as the political classes broadly held together whatever the popular nervousness. Ironically, the last Member

State to ratify was Germany, following a legal challenge to Maastricht which was rejected by the Karlsruhe Constitutional Court only on 12 October. Maastricht came into force on 1 November 1993, over a year behind schedule.

The Europe of Maastricht was a more bruised and uncertain body politic than had seemed likely when the treaty was signed. There was a strong school of thought, represented in Brussels and in Germany, that the answer to the doubters was to plough on with still greater determination. A series of policy papers from the German CDU[3] floated radical new ideas: these included the concept of 'core' Europe, with those who could not qualify for EMU being relegated to inferior status on the periphery, and the suggestion that the European Commission should itself be built up as a government for Europe.

The more common reaction was to slow down. In preparing the 1996 IGC foreseen at Maastricht, Member States sent delegates to a Reflection Group which quite effectively smoked out Member States' bottom lines and worked up a very moderate agenda for 'tidying up' Maastricht. The British delegate, David Davies, played a blocking role on nearly all proposals for deeper integration, at a time that the British government in any case found itself running a 'non-co-operation' policy as a result of EU measures forbidding the sale of British beef outside the UK. With the British government by now so divided it was close to paralysis in its European policy, some EU officials claimed they could not tell the difference between co-operation and non-co-operation. This 'phoney war'[4] continued until the election of Tony Blair's avowedly pro-European government, which took place on 2 May 1997, in convenient time for the Amsterdam Summit one month later.

It would be a mistake to suppose that these institutional dramas were the sum total of EU history following agreement at Maastricht. Part of the reason the years following 1992 were so disastrous for the Community institutions was overload. Apart from Maastricht, Member States had to cope with enlargement negotiations with a number of prospective candidates; with efforts to create a new relationship with the countries of Central and Eastern Europe; and with the long-running attempt to sign a world trade agreement to succeed the Uruguay Round. There was progress on all counts, but it was hard won.

In the autumn of 1994, there were referendums in Australia, Finland, Sweden and Norway on the membership terms offered by the EU. The Austrians and the Finns voted strongly for membership, then the Swedes narrowly in favour and the Norwegians narrowly against. The three new members joined on 1 January 1995. The Swiss, who had earlier expressed an interest in joining, withdrew after a referendum there rejected even the halfway house of joining the European Economic Area which would have linked it more closely to the Single Market.

Much time and energy went into negotiating Association Agreements with a number of Central European states, trying to bring them into a relationship with the EU that would lead to full membership one day. But critics suggested that the EU had become inward-looking, devoting too much effort to EMU and not enough to supporting the new democracies with the commercial and economic assistance they needed. Building up a new relationship with Russia and the Ukraine also preoccupied the Commission and the Member States; as did the negotiation of the Blair House Accord and the subsequent agreement on the World Trade Organization (WTO), which stretched relations to the very limit between the French and their partners.

Further, bitter disputes followed, with the British very publicly defending what they saw as their interests, both on arrangements for majority voting in the Council of Ministers, and on the successor to Jacques Delors. John Major decided to veto the candidature of the Belgian Prime Minister, Jean-Luc Dehaene, partly to please the Eurosceptic wing of the Conservative Party, but also in protest at what had been a clear Franco-German attempt to impose their candidate.

Yet, amid the acrimony, the EU was achieving its central goals. The French had been saved by the Bundesbank from speculation against the franc in summer 1993, with hard financial support which had not been offered to the British. The survival of the ERM at that point turned out to be more significant for the future of EMU than 'Black Wednesday' and there was a nice irony in the fact that it was the British Chancellor, Kenneth Clarke, who came up with the idea of 'broad bands' within the ERM, permitting greater currency fluctuations, as a way of keeping the system intact. The Madrid Summit of December 1995 approved the name of the Euro for the Single Currency. Following formidable attempts by Member States to meet the convergence criteria, some through the manipulation of national accounts, some with more substantive measures, the omens for a successful launch were looking up by the time of the Amsterdam European Council.

The Treaty of Amsterdam, agreed on 17 June 1997, was a modest affair. Tony Blair's government signed up for the Social Chapter. A new Chapter on Employment was added to the treaties. Certain institutional changes were made with a view to making the further enlargement of the EU more manageable: the scope of majority voting in the Council of Ministers was slightly expanded and the European Parliament had its powers mildly enhanced through the extension of the co-decision procedure. It was agreed that the Home Affairs and Justice pillar should gradually be absorbed – with delays and derogations – into the Community institutions and procedures. The Common Foreign and Security Policy was to remain essentially the province of the Member States – although a new and potentially powerful Secretary General position was to be created in Brussels to be its public face and to head the intergovernmental machinery.

Two developments early in 1998 turned out to be more important than Amsterdam. It was agreed in March that membership negotiations should be started with Poland, Hungary, the Czech Republic, Estonia and Cyprus. The implications for the EU of enlargement to this group of countries – very different in economic and geopolitical terms from the existing members – were enormous, in particular regarding budgets and foreign and security questions. After justified criticism that the EU had taken too long to act on the desire of the Central Europeans to 'return to Europe', there was now the serious prospect of a wave of new members arriving from about 2002 or 2003 on. And behind them was another cluster of actual and potential applicants, including Turkey and Ukraine, stretching to the borders of Russia.

Even more dramatic at the time was the decision on 2 May 1998 to go ahead with EMU on 1 January 1999, with all of the willing Member States who qualified under the Maastricht criteria: that is to say the original Six, with the addition of Ireland, Spain, Portugal, Austria and Finland. The Greeks expressed their intention of joining when their economy was ready; the British, Danes and Swedes continued to reserve their position, though Tony Blair's government had by now conveyed the impression that, subject to the successful launch of the Euro and a favourable referendum, Britain would join some time in the course of the next Parliament.

At the Brussels Council which agreed to proceed with EMU, there was a fierce Franco-German row over the presidency of the European Central Bank. This resulted in a messy compromise that the Dutch Head of the European Monetary Institute, Wim Duisenberg, should serve for the first four years then hand over to a French candidate, most probably the Central Bank Governor Jean-Claude Trichet, who would complete the eight-year term laid down at Maastricht. The agreement seemed to breach the spirit if not the letter of the treaty and fell into a familiar category of 'dirty deals' along the path of European Union. There could hardly be a better example of the continuing tensions at the heart of the EU between national and collective priorities. But, equally, there was no doubt that the collective political will was going to deliver on the prospectus once again. And the financial markets took the agreement in their stride.

Tony Blair's New Labour government held the EU Presidency through the dramas of EMU and enlargement, and seemed to be making some progress both in 'normalizing' Britain's relationship with its partners and de-dramatizing the European debate at home. The approach was to persuade people gradually of the practical advantages of EMU, should it work, and bring them round to a more sympathetic engagement with Europe. For their part, Chancellor Kohl and President Chirac were inclined to play down the integrationist push, partly because their political positions were both weaker than before, partly because they saw that this was the public mood. They submitted a joint letter to the Cardiff Summit in June 1998, calling for a

Europe more in tune with popular feeling and demanding a more rigorous application of subsidiarity. This would have been inconceivable even a year before. With the Commission keeping a much lower profile under its president, Jacques Santer, than it had under Delors, there was a feeling that the era of the institutional Great Leap Forward was over for the time being.

But, by now, it was also clear that turning the Euro from political decision into reality, at the same time as working out an overall strategy for extending the EU into Central and Eastern Europe, was going to be a huge task. The final destination to which this was all driving might not be very much clearer than it had been in 1945 or 1955. But in the course of two generations, the way Western Europe managed its affairs had been transformed.

The African businessman, mentioned at the beginning of this book, would be almost as confused today as he should have been in the 1950s about the prospects for Europe. But one could forgive him for being excited as well – however long he has had to wait for his catalogue.

Glossary

CAP Common Agricultural Policy

CFP Common Fisheries Policy

CFSP Common Foreign and Security Policy

COREPER Permanent Representatives' Committee in Brussels

EC European Community: the term generally used for the institutions of the EEC, ECSC and EURATOM from the time of the Merger Treaty in 1965. The correct term was actually 'European Communities'. It was only with the Maastricht Treaty that the EC became the formal term within the European Union for what had been the EEC – just as EU became the accepted abbreviation for the European Union as a whole.

ECB European Central Bank

ECSC European Coal and Steel Community

ECU European Currency Unit, used both as a unit of account for EC budgets and as 'basket' of European currencies within EMS.

EDC European Defence Community

EEC European Economic Community

EFTA European Free Trade Association

EMI European Monetary Institute

EMS European Monetary System

EMU Economic and Monetary Union

EP European Parliament

EPC Either European Political Community (early 1950s) or European Political Co-operation (1970s–80s).

ERDF European Regional Development Fund

ERM Exchange Rate Mechanism

EU European Union, established by the Treaty of Maastricht and comprising the European Community, which took on the functions of the EEC, and the 'pillars' dealing with CFSP and Home Affairs and Justice.

EURATOM European Atomic Energy Community

EURO Single currency unit which will be introduced on 1 January 1999 and put into circulation in EMU Member States two years later.

European Council Name for regular summit meetings of European heads of state or government: these took place irregularly until the 1970s, when they became thrice-yearly affairs, though since 1985 there are usually two meetings a year. Not to be confused with the Council of Ministers, at which all Member States are also represented, but which meets at any number of political or official levels to conduct the regular business of the EU in co-operation with the European Commission and the European Parliament.

Federalism Federations are usually political units with a central authority and jurisdiction applying to a number of subordinate units which might nevertheless have considerable autonomy. The EU has some federalist features, especially in the economic and commercial areas where there is clear Community competence. But the extent to which the EU should move towards an overall federal goal, in which the nation states are subordinate to the centre, remains deeply controversial. Those who support federalism often stress its decentralizing aspect (*see* 'subsidiarity').

FRG Federal Republic of Germany

GATT General Agreement on Tariffs and Trade

IGC Intergovernmental Conference
NATO North Atlantic Treaty Organization
OEEC Organization for European Economic Co-operation
Subsidiarity Principle derived from Roman Catholic theology that decisions should be taken at the lowest level at which action can be effective: means that local communities or, in EU, Member States, should take decisions which concern them and higher levels of authority should be involved only when necessary. Subsidiarity became especially important in the early 1990s in face of popular resentment of Brussels and was written into the Maastricht Treaty.
WEU Western European Union
WTO World Trade Organization

Notes

CHAPTER FOUR

1. According to Bernard Donoughue, Wilson's political adviser at
   the time: 'Mr Heath had taken the British Establishment into
   Europe. Harold Wilson took in the British people.' There is
   some truth in this at first sight unlikely statement. On the
   other hand, Wilson failed to end the split in the Labour Party,
   which subsequently became even more robustly anti-European.
   It would be more accurate to say that despite the polarization
   of positions within the political class, the referendum bought
   almost twenty years of public consent for Community
   membership as the framework for Britain's role in Europe.

CHAPTER FIVE

1. Malcolm Rifkind, the Foreign Office Minister for Europe,
   was present, representing the British Prime Minister, Mrs
   Thatcher. Following vigorous internal debate, the British
   decided despite their worries about the group to play a
   constructive part, protecting their position when they
   disagreed with the others by inserting footnotes in the final
   report. This disappointed some of the other delegates who
   would have preferred Britain to write a minority report –
   but in the event all delegations found reasons to enter
   footnotes and the report was agreed unanimously.

2. This article carried the further title, in brackets, of Economic and Monetary Union – which was adopted after initial German opposition, but showed clearly which way the traffic was headed.

CHAPTER SIX

1. The agreed solution was to revert in Article A of the Treaty of Maastricht to the wording of the Treaty of Rome, in creating 'an ever-closer union among the peoples of Europe' (*see* Glossary for the complications attaching to the word 'federalism').
2. It was not only the British Eurosceptics who resented what seemed to be growing intrusiveness by the European Commission on the basis of new Directives adopted under the Single Market Programme. Douglas Hurd, the 'pro-European' Foreign Secretary, had attacked the Commission's tendency to involve itself in 'the nooks and crannies of national life'.
3. The intellectual initiative lay very much with the CDU over this period: the working papers which party leaders like Wolfgang Schäuble, Karl Lamers and Rudolf Seiters published were drafted by a confident and formidable group of party activists with a very clear vision of how a closely integrated EU would serve both the European and the German national interest equally well.
4. It was a phoney war because Britain's partners were marking time until the arrival of a Labour government which they expected to be more co-operative. It was also rather good humoured: at the Florence European Council in June 1996, EU foreign ministers singing to Malcolm Rifkind on his fiftieth birthday cheerfully wished him a 'Happy Beef-day'.

Further Reading

This book is based mainly on secondary sources, on conversations with some of those involved in the story and on the author's own recent experience. But anyone with time to explore original archive material will find this a very rewarding approach – staff at the Public Record Office in Kew will be helpful with the abundance of material available there. To give one example, the internal Foreign Office minuting in 1950–1 on policy towards ECSC is fascinating in showing how the analysis of integrationist against intergovernmental arguments on Europe was conducted with almost exactly the same rationale, using just the terms, as in the debates in the mid-1990s. Some interesting exchanges can be found under the references FO 371 124962 and 124968.

Books which were useful in preparing this account and might be worth following up include the following:

Bainbridge, Timothy with Teasdale, Anthony. *The Penguin Companion to European Union* (Penguin Books, 1995). Clear, comprehensive, illuminating – outstanding English-language almanac.
Bond, Martyn, Smith, Julie and Wallace, William. *Eminent Europeans* (Greycoat Press, 1996). First-rate collection of essays on the main personalities involved.
Brivati, Brian and Jones, Harriet. *From Reconstruction to Integration* (Leicester University Press, 1993). Fine set of

analytical and historical essays; contributors include Richard
Mayne, Sean Greenwood and Lord Donoghue.

Charlton, Michael. *The Price of Victory* (British Broadcasting
Corporation, 1983). Examines the British dilemma, to join or
not to join. Detailed radio interviews with leading politicians
and officials of postwar years. A treasure-trove.

Colchester, Nicholas and Buchan, David. *Europe Relaunched*
(Hutchinson Business Books, 1990). Especially strong on the
making of the Single Market Programme, giving lively
account of the EC at the beginning of the decade.

Connolly, Bernard. *The Rotten Heart of Europe* (Faber and Faber,
1995). Heartfelt polemic on the politics of EMU from British
Commission official close to the dossier. Fascinating detail on
conflicts between national players.

Deniau, Jean François. *L'Europe Interdite* (Editions du Seuil, Paris,
1977). Corrective to cold-blooded Anglo-Saxon rigour. Passion-
ate, committed, often poetic account from a true insider.

Denman, Roy. *Missed Chances – Britain and Europe in the Twentieth
Century* (Cassell, London, 1996). Lively and polemical,
drawing on the author's direct experience as senior official of
the British government and the European Commission.

Duchêne, François. *Jean Monnet* (W.W. Norton and Co., 1994). Comprehensive and elegant insider's account from one of Monnet's
close British collaborators (Richard Mayne was another).

Grant, Charles, *Delors – Inside the House that Jacques Built*
(Nicholas Brealey, 1994). Powerful journalistic account,
drawing on interviews with the main players including Delors,
from *The Economist*'s then Brussels correspondent.

Greenwood, Sean. *Britain and European Co-operation Since 1945*
(Blackwell, 1992). Clear, incisive, especially good on
immediate postwar period.

Her Majesty's Stationary Office Documents on British Policy Overseas Series II (1986).

Jenkins, Roy. *A Life at the Centre* (Macmillan, 1991). Stylish and comprehensive account, often very funny. His Euopean diaries have more detail, but this is good for its national perspective as well.

McAllister, Richard, *From EC to EU, an Historical and Political Study* (Routledge, 1997). Invaluable for its Brussels perspective and a wealth of institutional detail based on close attention to documentary sources.

Mayne, Richard. *PostWar* (Thames and Hudson, 1983).

Mayne, Richard. *The Recovery of Europe* (Weidenfeld and Nicholson, 1970). Wise and authoritative, two rich and readable books showing Britain just failing to play its full part in a Europe in process of transformation.

Noble, Alexander. *From Rome to Maastricht, Essential Guide to the European Union* (Warner Books, Great Britain, 1996). Useful swing through the treaties and recent institutional developments.

Weidenfeld, Werner and Wessels, Wolfgang. *Europe From A to Z* (European Commission, Luxembourg, 1997). A practical mini-encyclopedia, translated from the German – detailed, accessible and well laid out. Available from European Commission Office.

Weir, Sir Cecil. *The First Step in European Integration* (Federal Educational and Research Trust, 1957). Practical study of ECSC by the Head of the first UK Delegation. A businessman's account, dry and factual, which becomes almost visionary in looking to the future of a developing federation of European states: 'The imagination cannot fail to be stirred and stimulated by such a prospect'.

Index

Bold type indicates more significant entries.

INDEX

INDEX